60 Supe[...]
If o[...]
a reaso[...]
— but not nee[...]
to know God.

75. Not care wh[...]
people think beca[...]
I interested in
unreliability of
human intelligence

87 — The little Bird

118 funny, tact
respectful but
difficult —
Seven
go forces

Spiritual Realism of St. Thérèse of Lisieux

Spiritual Realism

OF

Saint Thérèse of Lisieux

FROM THE ORIGINAL MANUSCRIPTS

BY

R. P. Victor de la Vierge, o.c.d.

TRANSLATED BY

THE DISCALCED CARMELITE NUNS

PEWAUKEE, WISCONSIN

THE BRUCE PUBLISHING COMPANY
MILWAUKEE

NIHIL OBSTAT:

Fr. Michael of the Holy Family, O.C.D.
Fr. Denis of the Holy Family, O.C.D.
Censores Ordinis

IMPRIMI POTEST:

Fr. Albert of the Blessed Sacrament, O.C.D.
Provincial

NIHIL OBSTAT:

John A. Schulien, S.T.D.
Censor librorum

IMPRIMATUR:

✠ William E. Cousins
Archbishop of Milwaukee
October 11, 1960

Library of Congress Catalog Card Number: 61–7492
© 1961 The Bruce Publishing Company
MADE IN THE UNITED STATES OF AMERICA

Introduction

"MY VOCATION, at last I have found it! My vocation is love! Yes, I have found my place in the Church, and this place, O My God, Thou Thyself hast given me: in the heart of the Church, my Mother, I will be love . . . thus I shall be all things!"[1]

Endlessly quoted, this statement remains inexhaustible in its depth. It expresses perfectly a most exalted ideal of St. Thérèse of the Child Jesus, one of the clearest lights that she received from on high.

But these ardent words do not only refer to her Carmelite vocation, to her role of contemplative in the world. They can also convey much to those whose tasks and way of life differ, for they clearly explain the universality of Thérèse's discovery and of her message. They stress the saint's intense theological life, a life which all God's children are called with her to share.

Let us admit that while Thérèse draws many souls, both within and without the Catholic Church, others are disappointed because, in reading her, they experience uneasiness over what seems to be a diluted Christianity.

The life of the saint presents some astonishing paradoxes.

After withdrawing from the world and leading an apparently insignificant life, she is declared to be the greatest saint of modern times. Pope Pius XI did not hesitate to proclaim her, a contemplative, patroness of all the missions. Despite her lack of outstanding literary gifts and her childlike imagination, she teaches a doctrine of astonishing richness, from which theology is deepened and spirituality renewed without either one having exhausted all its benefits.

What then is the underlying cause in these seeming contradictions? This: the life led by Thérèse and the "little way" which

[1] Ms. B, fol. 3 v°.

v

she reveals to souls are essentially theological. Now, nothing has a more unassuming appearance than the theological. Or, to be more exact, nothing embraces so well the substance of ordinary things nor expresses itself more happily through them, and nothing hides itself with so much joy beneath their surface, as the pure theological life. Occasionally, it is true, the supernatural breaks through the bounds of everyday life and bursts forth in outward, extraordinary phenomena but in that which is more substantial, it nourishes itself silently on whatever is offered to it even in the dullest of days. The life of man created by God, redeemed by Christ and transfigured by the Holy Spirit remains and must remain the life of a child of man, and the more this new life is profoundly divine, the more, also, it remains profoundly and simply human. Such is the elementary truth which places in relief the experience and teaching of Thérèse.

It is undoubtedly here that this child is truly modern, this child who never separates heaven from earth, either in her love or in her earnest searching for truth or in her daily preoccupations, and who never separates the concrete and changing conditions of her earthly pilgrimage from the demands of her divine vocation. Without doubt, it is also because she knows how to keep her life in balance and to bring it to fruition despite this conflict, that she has become the model of spiritual life for modern man.

Resembling great historical personages whose real lives have also, on a higher plane, a symbolic value, Thérèse is not only a very great saint, but she is the type of souls of our times, not only exclusively of the small number whom God calls to the cloister, but of all who are seeking their place in the Mystical Body, and who suffer in being always conscious of the limitations of their strength and the boundlessness of their desires.

Now, it is by the practice of her "little way" that Thérèse has come to find her place in the heart of the Church and that she has known how to remain there in an eminent degree. Therefore, to those who, despite their natural weakness, wish to fulfill their supernatural function in the world according to God's Will, it is important to understand well the theological foundations of this way which Thérèse has opened for them.

In order to facilitate the understanding of the Thérèsian message we have not believed it necessary to attempt a theological study of the saint's writings nor even a spiritual analysis, so to speak, of her experience. Work along these lines has been done successfully by others.[2] This attempt is conceived, rather, along the lines of a pedagogy of the theological and it presents to souls the progressive discovery and actual transmission by Thérèse of her ideal. Before this "little way" could be communicated to the world outside the cloister, the saint had to make it known to her companions during her lifetime. On May 17, 1925, Pope Pius XI had already stressed this fact: "(Saint Thérèse) has taught this 'Way of Spiritual Childhood' to her novices by word and example and she has made it known to all by her writings."

First, therefore, it is Thérèse finding her way and, second, Thérèse, guiding other souls in following it through the most varied and humble of circumstances, which we shall try to follow and make live again. But it is evident that our rather psychological and sometimes even pedagogical perspective should not make us forget the doctrinal elements upon which the saint so strongly depends: Scripture, the teaching of the Church, and the Rule and spiritual doctrine of Carmel. Likewise, our analysis of her spirituality and of the movement of abandonment so characteristic of her "little way," can be understood only with reference to the great underlying realities of the life of God and its communication to the soul by the Church and the sacraments. To repeat, our intention in these pages is not to return to these presupposed essentials.

Here, then, is the ground plan of this book. After a brief analysis of Thérèse's life in the environment of Carmel and of the spiritual atmosphere that she created and through which she worked to reveal her way of love to those around her (Chapter I), we shall attempt a study of her personal experience. First, we shall endeavor to make clear the intention which guided her in her spiritual search (Chapter II), and then follow, in sequence, her discovery of all the elements of her doctrine (Chapter III).

---

[2] Liagre, *Retreat With St. Thérèse of the Child Jesus;* Petitot, H., *St. Thérèse of Lisieux, A Spiritual Renaissance;* Philipon, M. M., *St. Thérèse of Lisieux;* Combes, *The Spirituality of St. Thérèse (an Introduction);* and other works.

We shall later show her way of teaching souls and of making available to them the fruit of her interior experience. Thérèse will begin by showing them the requirements of the "little way," the fundamental dispositions necessary for confidently entering upon it (Chapter IV). Next, the necessary steps of the child of God in its progress toward the Father will be brought to light: faith in Love, which is shown as the foundation of the way (Chapter V); then the offering to Love, the decisive engagement in this way (Chapter VI); finally, the practice of abandonment, which is the constant aim of the soul given up to love (Chapter VII).

In conclusion we shall link these various considerations to an idea very close to our saint: the heart of the Church (Chapter VIII), where created and Uncreated meet. This is the place to which the "little way" has brought Thérèse. In this vital sphere her soul has attained its marvelous theological fulfillment.

The Heart of the Church, a full expansion in confidence and love — these are the heights to which Thérèse wishes to draw after her a great number of souls.

Fr. Victor de la Vierge
Carmelite Monastery, Bernay (Sarthe)

Abbreviations Used in the References

Ms. A, Ms. B, Ms. C. . . . Autobiographical Manuscripts

S.S. . . . St. Thérèse of Lisieux, the Little Flower of Jesus: Definitive edition of The Autobiography, Authorized American Reproduction (1926), trans. by Rev. T. N. Taylor; P. J. Kenedy & Sons, N. Y.; containing "Counsels and Reminiscences," "Letters," Selected "Poems" and "Prayers."*

M. . . . A Memoir of My Sister St. Thérèse: by Sister Genevieve (Celine Martin), Authorized Translation of Conseils et Souvenirs; Trans. by The Carmelite Sisters of New York; M. H. Gill and Son Limited, Dublin, 1959.

N.V. . . . Novissima Verba: Rev. Trans. by The Carmelite Nuns of New York; Copyright 1952, P. J. Kenedy & Sons, N. Y.

E. . . . L'Esprit de Sainte Thérèse de l'Enfant-Jésus.

L. . . . Collected Letters of St. Thérèse of Lisieux: Edited by The Abbé Combes; Trans. by F. J. Sheed; Copyright 1949, Sheed & Ward, Inc., N. Y.

Sum. . . . Summarium of the Process.

Doc. . . . Documentation of the Carmel of Lisieux.

Circ. . . . Circular Letter of Sr. Marie of the Trinity of the Carmel of Lisieux, signed by Mother Agnes of Jesus, dated Feb. 20, 1944; Translation, "A Novice of Saint Thérèse" by the Carmelite Nuns of Allentown, Pa.; Copyright 1946.

P. . . . Poems of St. Thérèse of the Child Jesus: Trans. by the Carmelites of Santa Clara, Calif., U.S.A.; London, Burns Oates and Washbourne Ltd.; Reprinted, Nov., 1926.

NOTE: Scripture quotations from the New Testament are taken from the New Catholic Edition of the Holy Bible, Confraternity Edition. The Old Testament quotations are taken from Douay Version of the Bible.

---

* Although the Mss. are the first source, we give also the references to "St. Thérèse of Lisieux" to facilitate reading.

Translators' Note

THE quotations have been translated directly from the French and the references given are solely to refresh the readers' recollection. The references to the poems are taken from the *Poems of St. Thérèse of the Child Jesus,* inasmuch as the *Definitive Edition of the Autobiography* does not contain all of St. Thérèse's poems.

Some footnotes have been omitted because the sources could not be found; others which could not be found in the given source were quoted from another source.

No English translation being available of *L'Esprit de Sainte Thérèse de l'Enfant-Jésus,* the author's references were quoted directly. This book is a collection of classified selected documents and there is no author's name.

In the first chapters the author cites many quotations and examples in order to refresh the readers with the atmosphere of *The Story of a Soul.*

Contents

Appendix

The Practice

CHAPTER I

The Life of Thérèse at Carmel

WE ARE so accustomed to considering the personal aspects of the spiritual growth of St. Thérèse of the Child Jesus, first, in the bosom of her family and then in Carmel, that we seldom think of showing her in the role of teacher.

This is to forget that, except for the last months spent in the infirmary where she died, our saint remained in the Novitiate for all of her religious life, a little more than nine years, and during four of those years she was Mistress of Novices, although not officially invested with the title. This charge was given to her solely because of her increasing holiness. In this unusual situation the sanctity of Thérèse, as well as the strength and coherence of her message, may be assessed at their true value.

To rejoin Sister Thérèse in the Novitiate, therefore, is to come upon her in full strength, in the thick of the fray. Let us then, first of all, briefly sketch the environment in which she spent her religious life.

Thérèse made her Profession on September 8, 1890; normally she should have left the Novitiate three years later, but her two elder sisters, Mother Agnes of Jesus and Sister Marie of the Sacred Heart, had preceded her in the Carmel of Lisieux. As the custom of the time allowed no more than two of one family to be members of the same conventual chapter, Thérèse was excluded from the chapter and remained in the Novitiate. (Thérèse had, however, made her Final Profession and received the black veil.) She continued to assist at the daily instructions of Mother Marie de Gonzague and to ask permissions of her, like all the novices.

3

On February 20, 1893 — Thérèse being then twenty years of age — Mother Agnes of Jesus was elected Prioress; the former Mistress of Novices, Mother Mary of the Angels, became Sub-Prioress, while the former Prioress, Mother Marie de Gonzague, was appointed Procuratrix (Chief Portress) and Mistress of Novices.

The new Prioress asked her young sister Thérèse to assist the Mistress of Novices in her work. This was to entrust to her a delicate task since it required much tact and prudence to work with Mother Marie de Gonzague, who was sensitive and easily offended. Again, there was nothing official in this appointment.

In the Novitiate Thérèse had the title of "Angel" (the sister, usually the youngest novice, who attends the postulant for the first three days in Carmel) to two lay sisters: Sister Martha of Jesus, who entered Carmel on December 23, 1887, and was therefore older in religion than Thérèse; and Sister Mary Magdalen of the Blessed Sacrament, who entered on July 22, 1892. Sister Thérèse of the Child Jesus was thus expected to assist discreetly in the spiritual formation of her two companions.

Two years later, on June 16, 1894, when Sister Marie of the Trinity entered Carmel, the Mother Prioress gave her full freedom to talk to her "Angel" in all her difficulties, whether of a spiritual or of a practical nature. Soon two other novices were entrusted to Sister Thérèse: Sister Genevieve of the Holy Face, her own sister Celine, who entered September 14, 1894, and Sister Marie of the Eucharist, her cousin Marie Guerin, who entered August 15, 1895.

This was the situation during the triennium of Mother Agnes of Jesus. In the new elections on March 21, 1896, Mother Marie de Gonzague was again chosen as Prioress of the Community and she decided to continue also as Mistress of Novices. Mother Agnes discreetly advised that she have Sister Thérèse assist her as much as possible with the direction of the novices; and Mother Marie de Gonzague, who held the young sister in high esteem, gave her the responsibility of the Novitiate.

The changing mood of the Mother Prioress did not permit Thérèse to make plans for any length of time, nor was any stability assured her in this post. To these difficulties was added the youth of Thérèse who had to counsel, encourage, and even reprove, when necessary, novices older than herself. We see in what humanly unfavorable conditions the saint had to exercise her charge and that until her death. It is along this path, however, that she sanctified herself and did so much good.

The Novitiate of Carmel, it will be said, is a very restricted field of action. Certainly, in this uneventful and hidden life where all is centered upon the interior and where one seeks only the essential, the exterior necessarily loses its importance. But here, precisely, is where heroism is nourished, on the monotony of daily fidelity in little evangelical acts; and the value of the acts is not measured by their greatness but by the love which permeates them.

This poverty of framework, so exacting for the will, partly explains the saint's discernment and intuitive understanding of her own tendencies and those of her companions. Understood in this light, the examples given by Thérèse, insignificant though they may seem, demonstrate, by contrast, the richness of her intuitions and her understanding of the human heart. Furthermore, her experience and her teaching, founded upon very ordinary and commonplace things, can thus be transposed almost at will, so to speak, into any social and psychological environment. The widespread success of *The Story of a Soul* is a sufficiently eloquent testimony of it.

Indeed, the genius of Thérèse consists not only in her instinctive grasp of the fundamental laws of our being governing nature and grace but, above all, in her finding a very simple means of directing all toward God. The saint is not content to find and follow her "little way," but she has known how to draw souls after her and make them blossom in the supernatural atmosphere which she created around her.

Thérèse herself realized that God had given her an exceptional aptitude for leading souls. She confided to Mother Marie de Gonzague how surprised she had been to see herself charged, so young, with the formation of her companions.

"Mother," she writes, "perhaps you will remember that often the Lord is pleased to give wisdom to little ones. . . . You did not fear to tell me one day that the good God was enlightening my soul, that He was even giving me the experience of years."[1]

[1] S.S. p. 153; Ms. C, fol. 4 r°.

On the manner in which she understood and carried out her charge, we can study the saint herself in the testimony she left us. *The Autobiographical Manuscripts*, formerly *The Story of a Soul*, gives relatively few details of that which interests us in her teaching. When, toward the end of her life, under the order of Mother Marie de Gonzague, Thérèse wrote the pages which were to constitute her last manuscript, she had asked Mother Agnes, "On what subject do you want me to write?" Her elder sister replied, "On charity and the novices." Thérèse obeyed, but these chapters speak more of charity and the life of abandonment to God than of the novices. Her notes and letters to her novices, since they reveal her in action, are extremely valuable, as are the *Recollections* by Sister Geneviève.

The circular letter written by Mother Agnes after the death of Sister Marie of the Trinity in 1944 is also rich in information. Lastly, we can draw from the Summarium in the Process and from the manuscripts published by R. P. François de Sainte-Marie. We are deeply grateful to the Carmel of Lisieux for all that has been made available to us.

1. What Thérèse Brought to the Novitiate

Here the saint is in direct contact with the souls she is to form and lead to the interior of Carmel. It is not only a matter of enlightening their minds but also of stimulating their wills. A doctrine is not enough; a way of life must be imparted. This is the work of patience in which time collaborates with God and in which each detail has its importance, since each instant may be either an acceptance or a rejection of Divine Love.

As we shall see, that which Thérèse brings to her companions is Jesus Himself, Jesus shining through her. During four years lived in a never faltering will to progress, she will have gained the heights of consummate perfection and her novices will see her die of love in full course. Nothing much escapes these souls, inexperienced without doubt, but athirst for the Absolute, and they see the real depth of their sister and her union with God, especially since they have more frequent and closer contacts with her than with any other religious.

The novices are captivated by this radiant holiness which is not at all austere but of a delightful simplicity. They want to imitate Thérèse, who, in her humility, consents to be their model. Frequently, the young Mistress refers to this desire. She replies, for example, to a novice who is too much attached to sensible consolations: "Ask for consolations! If you really want to be like me you will say:

> 'Oh! fear not, Lord, that I'll awaken Thee,
> I await in peace the shore of heaven!' "[2]

"It seemed to me that she had all that was necessary to direct us and to make us become saints," testifies one of her novices. "We could see she lived everything she told us and this inspired us to imitate her."[3]

Solely by her union with God and without effort or affectation, Thérèse is a living example for her sisters. Moreover, despite her youth, holiness has given her "the experience of years."[4] Under the action of the Holy Spirit Thérèse has known a rapid maturing, both intellectual and spiritual. The intensity of her interior life of silence and solitude bears fruit in a rich knowledge of God's ways in souls.

At this early period, she is gifted with a solid, harmonious personality, whose natural possibilities are increased tenfold and wonderfully refined through the divine action. The novices feel that in her nearness to God she is near to them. So unhesitatingly turning to her, they ask the secret of her strength and amazing conviction.

Thérèse readily responds to their needs. There is no question which she has not already asked herself and to which she does not have the answer. The struggles, temptations, and all "these sad feelings of nature"[5] from which the novices suffer have been experienced by Thérèse who conquered them by grace. She understands, explains, and dispels their difficulties almost without being told.

"I understood everything very well," she writes to a novice. "It really is not necessary for you to give me many details."[6]

---

[2] P. "To Live by Love."
[3] Sum. Extract from the Dep. of Sr. Mary Magdalen of the Blessed Sacrament communicated by the Carmel of Lisieux.
[4] S.S. p. 153; Ms. C, fol. 4 v°.
[5] S.S. p. 171; Ms. C, fol. 19 r°.
[6] L. pp. 341–342.

But Thérèse is not only a model and experienced guide for the novices; she also brings them a personal and profound doctrine of life, the fruit of her prayer and union with God. That her sisters feel the certainty of her teaching is not without importance, for their young souls need to receive the solid support of her firm and expert direction.

"Tell me who taught you this 'little way' of love, that so gladdens the heart?" one of them asked the saint.

"Only Jesus. No book, no theologian taught it to me but I feel deep in my heart that I am right."

"I believe it to such a degree," her companion answered, "that if the Pope were to tell me that you were mistaken, I should not believe him!"

"Oh," exclaimed Thérèse quickly, "the Pope must be believed above all. But have no fear for if, when I get to heaven, I learn I have led you into error, I shall soon appear to you to tell you to take another route. But if I do not return, believe in the truth of my words."[7]

What then are the principal characteristics of the young Mistress' teaching?[8] Above all, fidelity to the spirit of the Order. It is in this spirit that Thérèse steeped herself and in which she lived during her years of suffering and seeking. Mother Agnes testifies that as soon as she entered Carmel, the little saint began studying the works of St. Teresa and St. John of the Cross. However, it cannot be said that she read all the works of her Holy Mother, although she often quotes them literally. The influence of the writings of St. John of the Cross is more apparent. During the years 1890 and 1891 she nourished herself almost exclusively on them.

Scripture — on which one must, according to the Rule of Carmel, meditate day and night — is the principal source of the "little way." From the earliest days of her life in religion Thérèse is deeply moved by what she hears or reads of the Word of God. A day comes when Scripture alone is sufficient for her. In any state of suffering, doubt, or longing the saint opens the sacred Book; Isaias, the Book of Wisdom, St. Paul or the Gospels then offer her the

---

[7] Circ. pp. 37–38.
[8] We shall study the substance in the following chapters.

living image that she is seeking and that expresses her own thought. This is akin to an unceasing union between the spiritual intuition of Thérèse and Revelation.

In keeping with Carmelite spirituality, Thérèse's teaching is wholly evangelical. Freed from human conceptions and from too narrow a framework, faithful and as simple as possible, it is the expression of the way that our Lord Himself opens to souls. This is what has given her teaching the universal value recognized by the Church and makes it so expansive. In the "little way" there is no rigid and uniform method to be followed by all. Adaptable to each soul, it asks only a personal adherence. St. Thérèse's novices do not feel constrained or in an unnatural setting. To guide, console, and direct them, their Mistress draws plentifully from the New Testament, the Psalms, the Prophets and the Canticle of Canticles. What procedure could put a soul more at ease and give her greater security?

Thérèse does not authoritatively impose her doctrine. She knows — and this is more fruitful — how to make it loved and desired by the novices. In urging them to follow in her path, she does not try to restrict their liberty in any way; she aspires only to place them under the special direction of the Holy Spirit and to lead them where He wills.

Thus, for the souls confided to her care, Thérèse is a model of sanctity and an experienced guide. With deep conviction she transmits her teaching to them. This is essential, for only life communicates itself. What is a "dead letter" for the giver will often be that for the receiver, but that which gives life to the soul of the Mistress enters, almost of itself, into the souls of the novices.

2. The Atmosphere of the Novitiate

Turned toward God and sustained by Him, Thérèse creates in the Novitiate a truly supernatural atmosphere, free, joyful, and strong. From the beginning she establishes souls in a relationship of mutual confidence which permits her novices to depend upon her for everything. "She speaks familiarly with the novices on what concerns them at the moment."[9] Thérèse wants them to open their hearts to her without restraint. "My beloved Mother, you under-

[9] M. pp. 2–3.

stand that with the novices all is allowed; they must be permitted to say what they think, the good as well as the bad[10] . . . without any restriction. . . . With a simplicity that delights me they tell me all the conflicts that I give them and what displeases them in me; in fact, they do not scruple more than if it were a question of someone else, knowing it gives me great pleasure when they act in this manner."[11]

This candor not only delights the humility of Thérèse but it gives peace to souls. The sole fact that they can voice what they are thinking liberates them and permits them to see themselves clearly. The saint desires, and rightly so, that the novices should be able to tell her everything, even the temptations which they suffered against their Mistress. This is a sign of perfect confidence, so necessary if direction be efficacious. But what humility such simplicity asks of the Mistress! When she thinks it necessary, Thérèse does not hesitate to reveal to the novices her own struggles and difficulties.

In many little delicate ways she wins their confidences. A novice writes: "When I was receiving direction from her and I had painful things to tell her, she led me to the miraculous statue which had smiled on her in her childhood and said to me, 'It is not to me that you are going to say what is painful to you but to the Blessed Virgin.' I did as I was told and she stood beside me, listening to me. Then having had me kiss the hand of Mary, she gave me her advice and peace returned to my soul."[12]

"She was very discreet," states another novice. "I could confide everything to her, even my most intimate thoughts. I had nothing to fear for she never repeated a single word, even in conversations with her three sisters."[13]

Nevertheless, to be able to tell her everything is not enough. Where is confidence if one expects but little in return? Because Thérèse desires only God, for herself and for her sisters, the novices know they can rely on their Mistress more than on themselves in their quest of God.

---

[10] S.S. p. 181; Ms. C, fol. 26 r° and v°.
[11] S.S. p. 181; Ms. C, fol. 27 r°.
[12] Sum. Extract from the Dep. of Sr. Marie of the Trinity.
[13] Sum. Extract from the Dep. of Sr. Martha of Jesus.

As for herself, the saint has confidence in the novices because she believes in Christ's powerful action in their hearts. Her wonderful knowledge of the working of grace in her own soul enables her to divine the souls' absolute need of God and the wonders they can do with His help. Thérèse believes in grace and in its support, even till the victory is won.

One of her novices was so beset with difficulties during her canonical year that everything seemed lost. St. Thérèse asked her, "Do you still have confidence that you will succeed?"

"Yes, I am so convinced that the good God will give me this grace that nothing can make me doubt it."

"Keep up your confidence," the Novice Mistress firmly replied, "for it is impossible that God will not answer you; He always measures His gifts in proportion to our trust. However, I admit that, if I had seen you weakening in hope, I, too, should have doubted it for, humanly speaking, there is no hope."[14]

In due time the novice made her Profession, convinced that she owed this priceless grace to her Mistress, who seemed, that day, as happy as she! Thérèse, with her supernatural intuition, judged her novice's vocation by the measure of her faith in God and not by her own determination to succeed.

But the atmosphere in which Thérèse has her novices live is not only that of total confidence but also of virility. The saint is very exacting. Ever prudent, she admits no compromise or half-measures which end in mediocrity. To too many people the religious life seems like an incubator for souls, a refuge for weaklings. Thérèse, who understands the life well, knows what it costs and how much this hard battle exacts even of well-balanced temperaments and strong characters. She teaches her novices to rely upon themselves for nothing, to leave all that is not God and always to forget themselves. Sister Genevieve reports, "She could not endure that importance should be attached to trifling discomforts."[15]

"I should like," she tells a novice, "always to see you a brave soldier, never grumbling at hardships but considering the wounds of your companions as most serious and your own as mere scratches."[16]

14 Circ. pp. 17–18.
15 Sum. Extract from the Dep. of Sr. Genevieve of the Holy Face.
16 M. p. 198.

The "little way" does not foster childishness. Thérèse often repeats that the novices are child-warriors, child-apostles, missionaries, and martyrs,[17] who should, consequently, not desire consolations, but should put away childish things[18] and learn to fight in the arena.[19] They should never place the blame for their faults on physical causes.[20] The way of childhood is for little ones but not for the fastidious or fainthearted. "You must practice the little virtues," explains Thérèse. "This is sometimes difficult but God never refuses the first grace which gives courage for self-conquest; if the soul corresponds to that grace, she immediately finds herself in the light. I have always been struck by the praise given to Judith (15:11): 'Thou hast done manfully and thy heart has been strengthened.' In the beginning we must act with courage. By this means the heart gains strength and we go on from victory to victory."[21]

She was fearless and strong like Joan of Arc whom she loved so much; neither spiritual trials nor sufferings could weaken the driving force within her. We would not have portrayed the Novitiate truthfully, had we not insisted on the joy that reigned there.

Thérèse did not like sadness; while yet a child she copied, as if by predilection, this saying, "A sad saint is a sorry saint." She refused to imitate the saints who were always serious, even at recreation. Thérèse herself was very gay. Her pleasant, lively, and sometimes witty conversation was the delight of community recreations. She wanted to find this same joy in her sisters: in their faces, in their words and, still more, in their souls. She reminds them: "Having willingly and freely embraced the Rule on the day of our Profession, we should certainly be inconsistent in acting as though the religious life were an unending, wearisome burden."[22]

Confidence, virility, joy — these are three dispositions which Thérèse thinks necessary in the formation of souls. At first glance these three elements may seem unrelated, but further thought reveals them as complementary. All three help to create one and the same atmosphere of openness. A confident soul is a soul that opens itself to another and offers itself to her supernatural influence.

---

[17] S.S. p. 296; L. p. 323; M. p. 142.
[18] L. p. 324.
[19] Cf. M. p. 142.

[20] M. p. 24.
[21] N.V. pp. 92–93.
[22] E. p. 204.

A virile soul, instead of falling back upon itself, forgets itself and spends itself in love. Joy is both the sign and the means of obtaining that detachment which springs up in a soul the moment it ceases to think of itself. Likewise, joy is the blessing of a heart captivated by love.

Thérèse's Novitiate is not a group that is restricted, nor is her doctrine based on an inflexible code. The saint instinctively places souls in the psychological conditions necessary to enable them to accomplish what is asked of them: not to remain on the level of their personal problems, living for themselves, but to live in Another and of the same life as that Other.

3. Thérèse and the Direction of the Novitiate

Nowhere in Thérèse's work do we find a "method" of direction for the Novitiate. When Mother Agnes asks her to speak of her task, she explains her approach to it by stating that her intention is to do all for God alone and the secret of her action consists in doing all through Him alone. Then follow very important psychological and spiritual observations, in no set pattern. Thérèse does not bind herself to a method. With her spiritual intuition and her sensitivity to shades of meaning, she has quickly seen that no standardized system is possible when one deals with souls and that no formula is suitable for all. She gives the avoidance of a system as the first condition of efficiency, and variety and flexibility as the means of formation.

"We feel," she writes, "that it is *absolutely* necessary to forget our tastes, our *personal ideas*, and to guide souls by the path that Jesus has traced for them, without trying to make them follow our own way[23] . . . I have already told you, dear Mother, that in teaching others, I have learned a great deal. From the beginning I realized that all souls have more or less the same battles, yet they are so different that I do not have any difficulty understanding what Père Pichon says: 'There are more differences among souls than among faces.' It is impossible to act with all in the same way."[24]

---

23 S.S. p. 176; Ms. C, fol. 22 v° and 23 r°.
24 S.S. pp. 177-178; Ms. C, fol. 23 v°.

Without the benefit of modern psychology Thérèse has grasped the great diversity of temperaments and characters, and the necessity of adapting herself to each individual soul so as to make herself truly and efficiently all things to all.

She also has observed that grace is poured into each soul according to a particular manner, and that souls are as different as bodies. In meditation she sought the reason why our Lord cultivates such a diversity of flowers in His garden.[25] One day she understood that it is their very variety that pleases God because it makes for the charm and beauty of the whole. It is not her desire, now that she is a gardener of souls, to make them all alike, to mingle the flower of the field with that of the garden, to cultivate every one of them in the same manner, or to prune and to gather all in the same season.

Thérèse's way is to follow the Holy Spirit and Him alone; therefore, she is usually lively and spontaneous. She improvises; she creates for each soul as God Himself does. We remember the charming story of the shell brimming over with the tears of the Sister who wept too much, of the top, etc. Thérèse does not like the rigidity of a system, of "accounts rendered" or of "practices." She binds herself to them in charity but does not hesitate to avow to Celine: "I am still obliged to have a chaplet of practices. I made it in charity for one of my companions . . . I am caught in a network which hardly pleases me."[26]

However, there is nothing soft in this attitude of Thérèse. The absence of standardizing methods is not an omission but a deliberate rejection on her part, prompted by her experience with souls. There is no lack of precise direction in her teaching, as a whole.

If the saint takes such care to adapt herself to each of her novices, it is because, above all, she sees in each one an irreplaceable soul, the object of the special love of Jesus.

In directing the Novitiate, Thérèse is not concerned with externals. Her principal object is to plumb the depths of the personality in which God works and desires to reign. Nothing superficial stops her; she corrects the externals only as they reveal or conceal the light within; nature occupies her only in its relation to grace.

---

[25] S.S. p. 30; Ms. A, fol. 2 r°.   [26] L. p. 196.

She goes directly to the essential, placing herself so as to see all things from the viewpoint of God.

That Thérèse, today canonized, almost a "doctor" in spirituality, should have assumed the role of Directress during her lifetime should not astonish us, seeing that the Carmel of Lisieux rarely had outside spiritual help. The Novice Mistress, in the measure in which a soul opens herself to her, can give that soul the fruit of her own grace and experience; the better she knows the inner life of the novice and her thousand ways of reacting to humble, daily realities, the more efficacious her guidance can be. However, all this is subject to the control of God's minister, to whom the novice always has a right to have recourse, as the Mistress often has the duty to do so.

If it is true that all souls should remain free, that one should not compel a manifestation of conscience by inducing painful confidences, it is no less true that the ideal Novice Mistress should be both a mother and a sister to her novices. They should be able to tell her everything; her advice should be followed with confidence and joy because they feel it is inspired by a most clear-sighted, discerning love. Charity must not remain locked up in a heart. Jesus said, "No one lights a lamp and puts it . . . under the measure, but upon the lamp-stand, that they who enter in may see the light."[27]

Thérèse, intimately docile to the Holy Spirit, possesses a remarkable knowledge of souls and of the supernatural life. She can recognize at a glance the delicate and obscure workings of the conscience. One would say that her intuition is so penetrating and her counsels so appropriate that she reads souls "like an open book." The novices often say to her: "But you have an answer for everything; I thought I would confuse you this time. . . . Where do you find what you tell us?"[28]

When one novice tries to hide her feelings from her, it is in vain: "Virtue shines naturally," said Thérèse (and that is true for her purified gaze). "I notice at once when it is no longer there."[29] "Some are even simple enough to believe I can read their soul

---

[27] S.S. p. 163; Ms. C, fol. 12 r°; Lk. 11:33.
[28] S.S. p. 180; Ms. C, fol. 26 r°.   [29] N.V. p. 64.

because at times I happened to make known to them — without their revealing it — what they were thinking."[30]

The young Mistress smiles at their amazement but admits, however, that she herself is "often astonished to see so clearly."[31] Whence comes this clear insight? It is not derived from a broad culture, for her fragile health and her entrance into Carmel at fifteen years of age did not permit her to complete even the ordinary course of studies, nor is it from a long acquaintance with people who could have refined her natural penetration. Thérèse has lived very little in the world and has hardly known it.

Could this experience be a result of much spiritual reading? Certainly, Thérèse is not unlearned in this regard. Her spiritual life rests on a very solid knowledge of Christian doctrine, in which she has been well instructed from the time of her childhood. She has had contact, as we have seen, with ascetical and mystical writers. But with what ease she frees herself from them! One has only to read her letters and her notes and to observe her with the sisters to see how little "bookish" she is and how little taste she shows for the abstract teaching of the masters. It is evident that this is not the primary source of her knowledge of God's ways in souls.

Does this knowledge come to her from charismatic gifts? No, indeed; Thérèse denies it. "I was very certain I did not have the gift of reading souls."[32] Her intuition is but the normal fruit of the Gifts of the Holy Spirit carried to a high degree of perfection and refined, so to speak, by the saint's faithful correspondence to them.

The more Thérèse is surrendered to divine influences, the more delicate her natural sensitivity becomes and the more penetrating her spirit in all that concerns the life of grace and its operations. Certainly, she recognizes "that in teaching others she has learned much,"[33] but she emphatically declares, "There is much that God alone can know in the depths of the heart."[34] However, she incessantly asks Him to feed His little ones and, in so far as it is necessary,

---

[30] S.S. p. 180; Ms. C, fol. 26 r°.
[31] S.S. p. 230; Ms. C, fol. 23 r°.
[32] S.S. p. 181; Ms. C, fol. 26 r°.

[33] S.S. p. 177; Ms. C, fol. 23 v°.
[34] S.S. p. 172; Ms. C, fol. 19 v°.

her union with Him allows her to share in the intimate knowledge He has of all His creatures.

"One night, one of my companions had resolved to hide from me a sorrow which was making her suffer very much. I met her the first thing in the morning and, with a smiling face, she spoke to me. Without answering her I said, with conviction, 'You are unhappy.' If I had made the moon fall at her feet, I believe she would not have looked at me with greater astonishment. Her amazement was so great that for an instant I was seized with supernatural awe. I was very sure that I did not have the gift of reading souls and was the more surprised that I should have guessed rightly. I felt truly that the good God was very near, for, without my being aware of it, I had said, like a child, words which were not mine but His."[35]

When the novices are surprised to see her reveal their innermost thoughts she explains: "Here is my secret. I never advise you without having invoked the Blessed Virgin. I ask her to inspire me to say what will do you the most good and I myself am often surprised at the things I teach you. I only know that in speaking to you I am not mistaken and that Jesus speaks to you through me."[36]

Thus from her union with God, Thérèse's direction derives its exceptional efficacy. It is a direction of delicate nuances difficult to define. Many of the saint's replies, many of her ways of acting and reacting would merit a detailed analysis. We shall only cite several distinctive features which are especially important.

The direction of Thérèse is both firm and flexible. It would be difficult to separate these two characteristics, for its firmness is not rigidity, nor is its flexibility vagueness or incertitude. Most important of all, Thérèse knows the goal to which she must lead souls, and she also knows how to help each one attain this goal. She teaches the novices how to consult, to listen to and to actually follow the Holy Spirit. Far from her, indeed, is the thought of having the Sisters end up with an imaginary "perfection" based on false exaltation and disguised self-love. Thérèse does not direct them toward

---

[35] S.S. pp. 180–181; Ms. C, fol. 26 r°.
[36] S.S. p. 230; Dep. of Sr. Marie of the Trinity on the Supernatural Gifts of the Servant of God: Sum.

an ideal they could create for themselves, but she encourages them
to be docile to the particular call of the Holy Spirit. She wants to
teach them to perceive the desires of God in the present moment
in order to be docile to them, that in this docility His direction
may become concrete, practical, and precise. For her, self-denial is
of more value than beautiful thoughts. She mistrusts excessive
mortifications in which there is more of nature than of virtue. Her
sister, Genevieve, exclaims: "Oh, when I think of all I have to
acquire!" Thérèse immediately corrects her: "Say rather to lose . . ."[37]
She teaches that it is better to lose than to gain; that is, to go deep
into the valley of humility and practice there the little virtues rather
than to strive for the glorious ascent to perfection.

Singularity is not permitted, nor complexity, affectation, or vagueness. Simplicity, truth: these denote the basic attitude for all, but
this attitude will manifest itself in a different way for each soul.
Difficulties and aptitudes vary according to temperaments and characters and Thérèse does not ask either the same efforts or the same
progress from each novice. In each particular case the saint gets to
the root of the matter and discovers the real state of the soul. She
ferrets out the weaknesses, the too natural instinct to forget and to
neglect the one thing necessary, and to complicate the spiritual life
by relying upon one's own strength. Thérèse always gives immediate
and effective help whatever the disorder, difficulty, or pain. Without
hesitation she touches the precise point to which attention and
effort should be given.

A novice comes to tell her, "I am discouraged at not being able
to imitate you in your tender love toward the good God."

The saint immediately perceives, not the apparent good will
which would have deceived a superficial observer, but a subtle
jealousy, and without hesitation she replies, "Each time you feel
this temptation, recite the following prayer: 'My God, I thank Thee
that I do not have a single tender sentiment but I am happy to
admire it in others.' " And she adds, in words of encouragement,
entirely supernatural, "This will be more pleasing to the good God
than if you were always irreproachable."[38]

"Very often," Sister Martha of Jesus confesses, "if I had followed

---

[37] M. p. 28.   [38] M. pp. 65–66.

my natural inclination I should have avoided seeking direction from the servant of God, knowing that my faults would be exposed. But her holiness attracted me so strongly that I went almost in spite of myself."[39]

St. Thérèse knows not only where to touch the soul but, what is more, how to touch it. To help the novices practice self-denial, to return to God after their infidelities and to cling steadfastly to His grace and to that alone. Thérèse knows how to temporize, thereby seconding the divine action and not anticipating it. Then she says what is necessary and as it is necessary. The young Mistress can be momentarily firm and severe with some of the novices, humble and gentle with others, but always just and true, neither exaggerating nor minimizing anything, and sometimes even simply laughing.

A novice who had just been reprimanded came one day, completely discouraged, to tell her Novice Mistress sadly, "I no longer have a vocation!"

To this solemn announcement Thérèse replied by laughing. How true it is that the Holy Spirit makes use of the most natural gestures of one whom He possesses! Thérèse, who was severe in the case of ill-humor or a melancholy whim, could not take the matter seriously and the trouble vanished. Since this incident, if something seemed to go wrong, the Mistress forestalled the tendency to discouragement by saying: "You no longer have a vocation today, is that right?" . . . And the trouble would disappear as on the first day.[40]

Thérèse constantly encourages her novices. To adapt herself to each one does not mean that she asks little of them. On the contrary she is, as we have seen, very exacting, but what ingenuity she employs to make souls expand, to establish them in a holy liberty, to assuage their wounds! If she energetically lays bare their miseries she, at the same time, shows them God, His mercy and His love; she always leads them back to Jesus. Her whole direction aims at this: to anchor the soul in God with a living faith, in the never-ending action which He exercises upon all our accepted miseries. In the midst of so many afflictions what could be more

---

[39] Sum. Extract from the Dep. of Sr. Martha of Jesus.
[40] Circ. p. 17.

comforting! To a novice who is tempted she explains: "Notice the method used to polish brass. First, it is coated with mud, which soils and tarnishes it. Then it is rubbed vigorously until it shines like gold. Temptations are like this coating, for they only serve to make the opposite virtues shine in the soul."[41]

Thérèse "always tells the truth" with the love and tenderness of Jesus. "Her decisions are very clear and just"[42] but she does not act as with authority; rather, she explains and persuades, careful to strengthen, not break, the bruised reed.

During Thérèse's illness the novices were seldom allowed to visit her. "One day," relates Sister Marie of the Trinity, who loved the saint very much, "filled with sorrow and conflicts, I went to the infirmary and gave vent to my complaints in front of another Sister. The servant of God scolded me severely for my lack of virtue and sent me away. But in the evening she sent me this note:

" 'My dear little Sister, I do not want you to be sad; you know what perfection I dream of for your soul. That is why I spoke so severely to you. I should have understood your struggle and tenderly consoled you, if you had not spoken of it aloud, but kept it in your heart as long as God wished. I have now only to remind you that henceforth our affection must be hidden.' "[43]

Thus, with endless precautions,[44] Thérèse seeks out the little spark of generosity which still smolders in the depths of the soul, the glimmer of good will, the longing for God which persists, despite the temptations, shadows, or fluctuations on the surface. She appeals to the novice's love for Jesus and she often inflames and draws her with her own ardor. One day a companion, who told her of the fear she had of losing God's grace because of daily small lapses, received this reply: "As the good God is all mercy and as you have good will, it is not you who lose but He Who is being deprived of love."[45]

This placing of the emphasis where it belongs makes us marvel at the penetration of Thérèse's mind and at her skill in teaching.

---

[41] Circ. p. 36.
[42] Sum. Extract from the Dep. of Sr. Marie of the Trinity.
[43] Circ. pp. 40–41.
[44] Cf. E. p. 82.
[45] E. p. 12.

Through these few words she not only banishes paralyzing fear but she arouses the purest and most unselfish love; the soul's gaze is turned from self and fixed wholly upon God. Will not the Sister thus strengthened fly with a new heart to sacrifice, so that Jesus may not be "deprived of love"?[46]

"Without sometimes acknowledging it," testifies Sister Genevieve, "all appreciated the direction of Thérèse, and although it was neither soft nor indulgent, they had recourse to it out of a natural need for truth."[47]

In this salutary atmosphere of candor, of supernatural and clear-sighted love, under the direction of a Mistress whose only desire is to be God's instrument, souls expand and develop toward their complete fulfillment. How could they forget lessons so full of life? Confidence, joy, and freedom: all co-operate to assure them a harmonious and personal development.

---

[46] E. p. 12.
[47] Sum. Extract from the Dep. of Sr. Genevieve of the Holy Face.

CHAPTER II

The Intention of St. Thérèse

IF THÉRÈSE knew how to create an even atmosphere for her novices, instilling a common ideal of sanctity and establishing union among them despite the diversity of characters and differences in their early formation, it is because her own spiritual life was dominated by one single thought. All geniuses and saints know that untiring pursuit of a great ideal which absorbs and unifies their whole existence. Geniuses conceive of this driving force as derived from personal intuition, whereas for saints it is born of a truly divine inspiration, faithfully obeyed, meditated upon and deepened each day.

The great ideal of Thérèse, the inmost expression of the divine will in her soul does not bring division into her life. Her duty as teacher does not distract her from her quest of God; she makes it part of that quest, for the saints do not have two objectives; they remain faithful to their inspiration while striving their utmost to share it with others.

Thérèse unequivocally declares what her fundamental idea is, and her conduct confirms this testimony. She has but one desire: TO LOVE JESUS AND TO MAKE HIM LOVED.

"I beg of you," she writes to a Sister at the Carmel of Saigon, "ask Jesus that I, too, may love Him and make Him loved."[1]

"I would love Him with no ordinary love but like the saints who committed follies for Him."[2] And to Brother Simeon: "*The only thing I would beg of you to ask for me is the grace to love Jesus and to make Him loved as much as I possibly can.*"[3]

---

[1] L. p. 328.   [2] *Ibid.*   [3] L. p. 310.

This is the main thought in all the letters of the saint's last years, and it is the central purpose which pervaded her whole life and directed her work with the novices.

A brief study of this dominating thought, its origin and development throughout St. Thérèse's spiritual life is necessary here, if we are to understand more fully its importance in her work as Novice Mistress.

1. The Search for "Jesus Alone" in the Life of Thérèse

No one would dedicate his life to a single value if he had not understood beforehand, with the realism of St. Thérèse, its urgency and soundness. If, at the age of twenty, Thérèse, in her duty and in her daily life, is oriented in an apparently extreme manner toward God alone, it must be because she has had a profound experience of Him.

Actually, this experience, given to her when a child, became more convincing day by day. It filled her mind, captivated her will and heart and satisfied her whole being as only the reality of God can.

Naturally very gifted, Thérèse spontaneously loves the great and the beautiful.[4] She has a spirit of delicacy, a clear insight, which enable her to go directly to the depth of things without being deflected by appearances. Her faith, received in the bosom of an exceptionally Christian family, illuminates still more her natural clear-sightedness. From the early awakening of her reason we see the child aware of the Allness of God and the vanity of the creature apart from God. She has, as though by instinct, the certitude that a St. Augustine and others acquired by an often long and sorrowful experience: all that is not God passes, all that passes is *nothing*, and this nothing leaves our heart absolutely unsatisfied when it tries to nourish itself upon it.[5]

Thérèse has drawn this knowledge from seemingly insignificant things: the "old and rancid" jam,[6] the little day-old lamb that dies, etc.

---

[4] S.S. p. 89; Ms. A, fol. 46 v°.

[5] These words as in other similar passages (pp. 28; 34; 66, fn. 6; 67, fn. 8; 76, fn. 45) are to be taken in a mystical sense: the creature is nothing outside of God; it is pure relation with Him.

[6] S.S. p. 46; Ms. A, fol. 14 v°.

"You do not know, dear Godmother, how much the death of this little animal has made me think. Oh! We must not be attached to anything on earth, even the most innocent things, for they are gone at the moment when we least expect it. Only the eternal can satisfy us."[7]

A mere trifle leads great souls to reflection. In the life of Thérèse, lowly incidents became great because of the greatness of the way she regarded them; great also was the heart which was deeply moved at their contact. Through her own small universe the child experienced the world, touched with sadness because of its limits; and it kept her heart hungry for something else.

This is not the simple melancholy of an orphan but the fruit of a real grace; Thérèse was in the school of God where the Master interiorly revealed to her the science of the saints and spoke to her heart in details adapted to her years. Recalling the time in her childhood when, in the solitude of her alcove, she "thought" of the swiftness of life and of eternity, Thérèse declares: ". . . I understand now that I was praying without knowing it and that the good God was already teaching me in secret."[8]

THE DESIRE TO LOVE JESUS AND TO MAKE HIM LOVED AT ANY PRICE

God is All, and truly that which passes does not merit the attachment of the soul. But who, having experienced this terrible devaluation of the creature before the reality of God, would not run the risk of despair? Or would he not end by relegating this certainty to the realm of the abstract, that he might live, indeed, as if he knew nothing about it?

Truly, man has something else. Between the sublime All of God and his own deceptive nothingness, there exists a most living, real, and mysterious bond: love. Because she has known God's love for her, Thérèse's first intuition becomes an ardent, absolutely irresistible conviction. Especially on the day of her First Communion Thérèse experienced love.

---

[7] L. p. 44.
[8] S.S. pp. 72–73; Ms. A, fol. 33 v°.

"Oh, how sweet was the first kiss of Jesus to my soul! . . . It was a kiss of love; I felt that I was loved."[9]

From that time on, what she *knows* — the All of God and the nothingness of all else — and what she *feels* — the Infinite love by which she is personally loved — leads her to turn toward God alone, to offer herself entirely to Him and to love only Him: "I love Thee; I give myself to Thee forever."[10]

The outcome of this deep and rapid development is a definite call to the life of Carmel. The divine invitation was heard by the little girl at the age of two and a half.[11] But it is only on a day in September or October, 1882, that the call becomes irrevocably definite: "I felt that Carmel was the desert where God wished me also to hide . . . I felt it so strongly that there was not the slightest doubt in my mind."[12] The child is so convinced of this call that she immediately speaks of it to her elder sister and to the Mother Prioress as well.

"To be for Jesus alone"[13] was the rigorous logic which was whispered in Thérèse's heart; it seemed to her that in the religious life she could realize this desire most perfectly.

It appears that there is nothing as yet, near or far, to prepare Thérèse for the apostolic life. The heart of the little girl is turned solely toward God. Well, it is also from Jesus that love for others will come to her, for love comes from God. Truly, by the grace of Christmas,[14] God had already opened to the world this heart that was His alone; but it is by the grace of July, 1887, that He clearly manifests it and gives her a sense of the Redemption. Since that day when she saw the Blood of the Crucified shed in vain, Thérèse burns with love for souls; but she loves and wants them for Jesus alone. He alone is the source of her consuming zeal; to Him alone would she bring sinners washed in His Blood. "The more I gave Him to drink," she writes, "the greater became the thirst of my poor little soul, and this ardent thirst that He gave me was the most delicious drink of His love."[15]

---

9 S.S. p. 74; Ms. A, fol. 35 r°.
10 *Ibid.*
11 Cf. S.S. p. 36; cf. Ms. A, fol. 6 r°.
12 S.S. p. 59; Ms. A, fol. 26 r°.

13 L. 113.
14 S.S. p. 86; Ms. A, fol. 45 r°.
15 S.S. p. 89; Ms. A, fol. 46 v°.

Rarely, perhaps, has the anguish of souls been, if not felt, at least expressed, in a more intimate, more profound relation with the sole love of Christ the Savior. It is a burning and terrible love which carries one away. To appease the thirst of her Beloved, Thérèse wants souls: "As yet it was not the souls of priests that attracted me, but those of great sinners; I burned with desire to snatch them from the eternal flames . . . I wanted at all costs to prevent him [Pranzini] from falling into hell."[16] At all costs means for her at the price of the greatest generosity.

She sets herself, then, to love suffering, to find her joy in it. We see her throughout her life courageously accepting the trials which befall her, ceaselessly desiring the cross, even choosing it, under the form of a thousand daily little sacrifices. Whatever its outward appearance, henceforth suffering has for Thérèse an apostolic meaning and value. So much so that before dying she can exclaim: "I should never have believed it possible to suffer so much! . . . I can explain it only by my ardent desire to save souls."[17]

Thus the saint, who knows what God has accomplished in her, does not hesitate — on her deathbed — to identify the immensity of her suffering with the zeal which devoured her. And whoever is an apostle, whoever is charged with souls, can convince himself, with Thérèse, that to win a single soul, to see divine grace descend into a single soul, it is necessary to suffer much, to deny himself much and to embrace and lovingly carry the cross. The cross is the testimony of the love of the Master, as of the love of souls.

By Fidelity to Her Own Vocation

Called to divine union and to the sorrowful motherhood which is fraternal charity, how will Thérèse respond to the invitation of Jesus? By heroic fidelity to the vocation which she has received, in its deep spirit and in the letter, and that at every moment. As a matter of fact, by this fidelity alone can such a grace be maintained and stabilized; it is too often lost or wasted by less attentive hearts.

Thérèse knows herself called to Carmel; she is about to enter.

---

[16] S.S. p. 88; Ms. A, fol. 45 v°.   [17] N.V. p. 139.

She is completely aware that her vocation is a vocation to the purely contemplative life; her ardent and supernatural apostolic zeal, far from being an obstacle to this life, is in reality one with it.

Despite her desire to spend herself in apostolic works, Thérèse obeys the divine call which will separate her from everything, because she is confident of the promises of Jesus; her fidelity to God will be more useful to souls than an activity which He does not will for her. She does not renounce one or the other of her two loves. They are, on the contrary, so intimately one in her heart that she can say impartially: "I wish to hide myself in the cloister to give myself entirely to God,"[18] and: "Having bidden the world an eternal farewell, my one aim was to save souls, especially the souls of apostles."[19]

God does not disappoint Thérèse nor deprive her of anything. Quite the contrary. In her fidelity to the first love the saint will better discover the dimensions of the other. For the spouse of Christ, love of one's neighbor is inseparable from love of God: "The more I am united to Him, the more also I love all my Sisters."[20] "When a soul lets herself be captivated by the intoxicating odor of Thy perfumes, she cannot run alone; all the souls she loves are drawn in her train, freely and easily, as a natural consequence of her attraction toward Thee."[21]

Faithful in her apostolic ideal to her sublime vocation, Thérèse is no less so in the choice of the means employed by her ardent zeal. The first and greatest is the complete fulfillment of her duty of state. She does not want to let pass any sacrifices resulting from the observance of the Rule and she wants to live her religious life in all the fullness of its demands. By lovingly doing at every moment all that is required of her, she intends to radiate on souls near and far.

Whether we remember her worn out with fatigue and "walking for a missionary,"[22] or whether we see her accepting with admirable courage and peace her cruel trial against faith and thinking of un-

---

[18] To Celine: Mgr. Laveille, p. 140; E. p. 26.
[19] L. p. 294.
[20] S.S. p. 163; Ms. C, fol. 12 v°.
[21] S.S. p. 190; Ms. C, fol. 34 r°.
[22] S.S. p. 215; words spoken by Sr. Marie of the Sacred Heart. Sum.

believers,[23] everything in Thérèse's life and work seems colored with this zeal for souls which sets her heart on fire, as does the love of Jesus. And, above all, at each instant she has recourse to the infallible means: prayer! She fills her life with it.

Thus she remains steadfast in her soul's attraction: what she wants to give to souls is nothing less than Jesus and to Jesus nothing less than souls. This is a wholly supernatural end to which, of itself, no earthly manner, word or way of man can attain. One cannot impart God nor can one prevail upon Him. But love can incline Him who is Love to give Himself — this He waits for and desires.

Such is Thérèse's plan: above all, she uses the apostolic instruments par excellence supplied by her vocation, and she strives to remain as closely united as possible with the will of God. In so doing she unknowingly prepares herself for her work as teacher, for, before being a guide and support to others, she must be fully and for Jesus alone what He wants her to be.

2. The Search for "Jesus Alone" in Her Contacts With Souls

As Thérèse appears to us in her life, so do we find her in her role as teacher, or in her love for souls afar, as well as for those directly entrusted to her. How could she seek other than Jesus in her work with her young Sisters? There, more than elsewhere, she strives only "to love Him and make Him loved."[24] Let us see her at work in her search for the Beloved in the midst of her new duties.

Thérèse's ministry, like her life, is hidden. This does not displease her. She labors in silence and humility to unite herself to the Master, that He might reign in her soul and in those whom she directs. She knew that God could have done without her: "Why should I wish God to use me rather than another? Of what importance is the instrument provided He reigns over souls? Besides He has no need of anyone."[25] It was this very detachment which made her a perfect instrument in the hands of the Divine Artist.

---

[23] S.S. p. 156; Ms. C, fol. 5 v°.
[24] L. p. 312.
[25] N.V. p. 61; M. p. 205; cf. Phil. 1:18.

Thérèse exercises her duties with an entire submission and deference to her Mother Prioress, upon whom she depends for everything. This is not without merit, considering the great difference in the temperaments and souls of Thérèse and Mother Marie de Gonzague. Here again the saint finds good in meeting contradiction and the cross. Her conduct was so perfect that after her death the Prioress gave her this eloquent testimony: "A perfect model of humility, obedience, charity, prudence, detachment and regularity, she fulfilled the difficult obedience of Mistress of Novices with a wisdom and perfection which nothing could equal save her love of God."[26]

When her Mother Prioress or the community reproached Thérèse and complained of the little progress made by the novices, the young Mistress profited by these occasions to accuse herself and accepted the advice given her as though it came from God. "She never spoke of her vexations and annoyances . . . but in her difficulties put her whole confidence in God."[27]

The Holy Ghost was also teaching her in delicate situations always to act conscientiously for the good of souls and the interest of God, facing, when required, the reproaches of superiors or the complaints of the novices. She never acted on her own authority to serve her own interests; she was much less concerned with asserting herself than making herself a servant of her Sisters and loving her neighbor as Jesus loves him and will love him to eternity.[28]

Quoting the Gospel, she said, "Give to everyone who asks of thee and whoever forces thee to go for one mile, go with him two."[29]

Moreover, never did her charge serve as a pretext for Thérèse to permit herself the least infidelity to the Rule. Responsible for her Sisters, she is first of all a Carmelite, and her punctual submission to the observances and to the least customs increases. "I was forced to practice what I taught," she writes.[30] Faithful to her

26 L. p. 274, ref. 23.
27 Sum. Extract from the Dep. of Mother Agnes.
28 Cf. S.S. p. 163; Ms. C, fol. 12 v°.
29 M. p. 155; cf. Lk. 6:30; Mt. 5:41.
30 S.S. p. 171.

duty, Thérèse intends to be faithful in every obligation and to maintain a fully supernatural conduct. Thus, convinced of not being able to do any good outside of obedience, she firmly refuses to listen to a novice the moment the bell rings for prayer,[31] or interrupts another who, in receiving direction, tells her useless things. "We are both wasting our time. Let us go!"[32] Seeking only Jesus, Thérèse cannot permit the least selfishness in her love for her young Sisters: "I am ready to give my life for them (the little lambs)," she writes, "but my affection is so pure that I do not wish them to know it."[33] Undoubtedly, Thérèse sincerely loves her novices just as they are with their good qualities and their defects; she loves them with the same love that Jesus pours into her heart to draw them to Him. Her own heart is undivided because her charity, full of maternal tenderness and solicitude, springs naturally from her love of the Master. The novices "feel in the depth of their hearts that she loves them with a real love."[34]

Nor does the saint seek to be loved for herself. In guiding the novices in her charge, she never attempted to gain their affection by concessions of human prudence. She sought only their religious perfection, even at the expense of her popularity. Mother Agnes declares: "A hundred times I have seen her fidelity to conscience in dealing with the novices."[35]

Sister Martha of Jesus says, "Her zeal on my behalf and on that of the other novices was most pure and disinterested. When she was obliged to reprove us, she was not afraid to displease us and risk losing the popularity and the affection that indulgence toward our failings might have brought her."[36]

Yet Thérèse does not refuse pure affection, for she realizes it has an essential place in the direction of souls. Speaking of one of her "daughters," Thérèse writes to her sister Celine, "She is good and she loves me";[37] but she works untiringly to purify this affection and to strengthen the hearts of the novices. She intends to direct

---

[31] S.S. p. 318.
[32] Sum. Extract from the Dep. of Sr. Mary-Magdalen of the Blessed Sacrament.
[33] S.S. p. 177; Ms. C, fol. 23 v°.   [36] Sum.
[34] S.S. p. 177; Ms. C, fol. 23 r°.   [37] L. p. 236.
[35] Sum. pp. 561, 562, 1552.

them only toward God and the authority representing Him. "I have never, with the grace of Jesus, tried to draw their hearts to myself. I have understood that my mission was to lead them to God, and to make them understand that here below, you, Mother, are the visible Jesus whom they (the little lambs) must love and respect."[38] Her own testimony reveals how watchful she was that the love of her Sisters for their Prioress might be truly supernatural. To God alone Thérèse wishes to give her Sisters. Charged with the formation of religious souls, spouses of Christ, she knows that it would truly be a theft to take for herself a little of their natural affection, a truly cowardly, mercenary thing to let them fix their eyes on anyone but Jesus. Her certainty comes from having sounded the depths of her vocation, the Master's demands on the hearts of His spouses, and the happiness one knows in turning one's whole being toward Him.

Thérèse aims at God with a purity so uncompromising that her aim is not "to do good" to souls, to make them understand a given thing or to see them advance under her care. For God alone does she work and from Him alone does she expect effective results.

Thérèse completely reveals herself to Sister Genevieve in a valuable confidence: "The time that I spent with the novices was for me a life of war, of struggle. God worked for me and I worked for Him and never had my soul made such progress. . . . I did not seek to be loved; I did not worry about what people said or thought of me. I strove only to do my duty and to please the good God without any desire that my efforts should bear fruit. We must serve God and love what is good without anxiety as to what comes of it. To us, the work; to Jesus, the success. We must never fear the battle when it concerns our neighbor's welfare, nor fear to reprove at the cost of our personal peace, nor seek merely to enlighten the novices; we must always work only to serve God and leave the success to Him."[39]

To us it may seem that the saint carries detachment too far. Is it wrong to try to do good? Was not that her obligation? Unquestionably, Thérèse is not sparing in anything that might sustain,

---

[38] S.S. p. 177; Ms. C, fol. 23 v°.   [39] Sr. Genevieve (Sum.)

enlighten, form, and even console her Sisters. She spends herself for them without reckoning, but not for her own satisfaction nor to obtain a given result. She very simply wants to do her duty without a shadow of selfishness. This attitude alone permitted her to exercise her zeal untiringly; not hoping for success, she was never disappointed at not obtaining it.

Thérèse is not subject to weariness, discouragement, or any possibility of preferring a responsive soul to another less gifted, of doing more for one than for another. All the souls God has entrusted to her have the same right to her love and care. "If we find a soul displeasing to us, let us not repulse her; let us not ever abandon her. We always have 'the sword of the Spirit' to help her to amend her faults; let us never let things go to preserve our own peace; let us fight without rest, even without hope of winning the battle. What does success matter! Let us steadfastly go on, no matter what the weariness of the struggle. . . . We must do our duty to the end."[40] Thérèse is ready to risk everything, to expose herself to criticism for the good of souls. "Whatever happens," she promises, "I will tell you the truth! I would rather be obliged to leave the community than allow a soul to remain in ignorance."[41]

Prayer and penance remain her chosen weapons. Not without difficulty does she act with such integrity and zeal, does she watch over her young Sisters and reprove them for their faults. "But I feel it is very necessary that this should be a suffering to me," she confesses, "for when one acts according to nature, it is impossible that the soul whose faults are disclosed would understand that she is wrong.[42] It is true for me in this as in all else. . . . So, when I speak with a novice, I try to mortify myself when doing it . . . for it seems to me that we can never do any good when we seek self."[43]

Thérèse put these principles into practice with such perseverance that Sister Genevieve could declare at the Process of Canonization: "The whole strength of our young Mistress lay in complete de-

---

[40] S.S. pp. 324–325.
[41] Sum. Extract from the Dep. of Sr. Mary Magdalen of the Blessed Sacrament.
[42] S.S. pp. 176–177; Ms. C, fol. 23 r°.
[43] S.S. p. 177; Ms. C, fol. 32 v°.

tachment. She forgot herself completely and was always on the alert to mortify herself."[44]

Celine was not the only one to say this. The integrity of Thérèse's life impressed all her novices. All sensed the undeniable grandeur that a purpose so intensely divine gives to a consecrated life. Witness this admiration of a young Sister who one day knelt before her Mistress, joined her hands, bowed her head and exclaimed: "Oh, Sister Thérèse of the Child Jesus, you are not like the others! I am sure that after your death we shall kneel before you and say, 'St. Thérèse of the Child Jesus, pray for us.' This drew a friendly reprimand from the saint: 'What a child you are! Come now, you are making fun of me!' "[45]

By her conduct, more than words or action, their Mistress gave the novices the most necessary and fruitful teaching.

---

[44] Sum. pp. 210, 415.
[45] Circ. p. 37.

CHAPTER III

The Secret of Thérèse's Action

"JESUS alone!"[1] to love Him and make Him loved, by fidelity to her personal vocation — this is the intention controlling and vivifying the thoughts of Thérèse, Mistress of Novices. On earth this is her goal at any price; she rejoices that in heaven she may continue to fulfill it. How does she set about realizing her plan; how does she work without ever taking her eyes from Jesus? What is the secret of Thérèse's astonishing success? This is what we now propose to study.

Thérèse had already found the way to attain her own sanctity when she described it to others. Hence, to understand Thérèse as a teacher, it will be useful to look at the earlier experiences which led to her discovery of the "little way."

1. The Secret of Thérèse in Her Life

Thérèse admits that she did not immediately discover the way of spiritual childhood. She groped and searched; she suffered; but most of all she prayed.

During her entire life Thérèse seems especially diligent in doing everything she can. She gives herself unreservedly to Jesus; her fidelity to divine grace is such that one day the saint could admit: "From the age of three I have never refused the good God anything."[2]

She never uses her weakness as an excuse to avoid an effort. Whatever her littleness, she wants to give full measure, to comply with all the demands of God, to respond to all His advances. "I

---

[1] P. Title of a Poem; see p. 39, ref. 2.
[2] S.S. p. 298.

always strive to act as if I had made it [the vow of perfection]. I do not understand why a soul who loves God, and especially a Carmelite, can act otherwise, for this is a duty of our vocation."[3]

Thérèse says that she has not accomplished "the actions of the saints,"[4] but during her whole life and to her last days, she has given to Jesus, moment by moment, what she could give; she is *"a very little soul who can offer to God only very little things."*[5] There is nothing extraordinary in her works and sacrifices except the delicacy of a love which lets nothing pass without offering it.

"At my death," she says, "when I shall see the good God overwhelming me with His tenderness for all eternity, and I shall no longer be able to make sacrifices to prove my love for Him, I could not endure it if I had not done all that was possible to please Him while I was on earth."[6] And this she accomplished.

The limited place given to exterior mortification, the absence of extraordinary actions and some of Thérèse's own words should not lead us to minimize the "little way." Whoever meditates upon *The Story of a Soul* readily discovers the thorns, despite the ardor with which Thérèse gathers them, and the roses which hide them. The way of childhood lies where Thérèse wanted it, at the antipodes of paralyzing quietism and presumptuous confidence.

To a novice who spoke one day of her desire to share the little doctrine with her parents and friends, the young Mistress quickly replied: "Oh, be very careful in explaining it because our little way, misunderstood, could be taken for quietism or illuminism. Do not think that it is a way of repose!"[7] It was far from that for Thérèse.

Striving to accomplish everything to please God, the saint finds a negative and a positive side in this practice. Daily she sees more clearly her extreme helplessness in sanctifying herself or in accomplishing what God expects of her; yet at the same time, she experiences the efficacy of the divine action in performing the impossible in her.

---

[3] Dep. of Sr. Marie of the Trinity quoted in her Circ. Ltr.; Circ. p. 34.
[4] N.V. p. 94; cf. Ms. A, fol. 75 v°.
[5] S.S. p. 187; Ms. C, fol. 31 r°.
[6] E. p. 48.
[7] Quoted by Père Petitot in "Une renaissance spirituelle," p. 193. Cf. Circ. p. 38.

Even as a child, Thérèse was humble. Despite her voluntary dependence on God, she felt the strain between her aspirations and her daily accomplishments. Her powerlessness was painful to her, as ours is to us. Thérèse knew much sorrow and anguish: two years of debilitating scrupulosity; a secret fear of having lied when she told of her miraculous cure, despite her first intention to keep it a secret; the fruitless struggle against extreme sensitiveness and uncontrollable tears — all this simultaneously from early childhood until she was fourteen. Hard though it was to bear, this suffering deepened her humility.

In each of her failures or in the heartache of her inner misgivings, Thérèse is sorrowfully aware of her nothingness. However, God does not let her suffer in vain nor forever. Seeing herself delivered from her trials by Him alone, Thérèse acquires this deep conviction: God at last accomplishes in us what we come to understand He wants of us; our unaided efforts are utterly in vain. The grace of Christmas, 1886, is especially fruitful and full of peace. Thérèse writes: "Satisfied with my unfailing good will, Jesus did in an instant the work I had struggled for ten years to do."[8] From this moment on, particularly, the certainty of God's omnipotence on her poor nothingness is strengthened in her soul.

However, she will have much to suffer before knowing what the embrace of Jesus is in a surrendered soul, before He establishes her in confidence and in unwavering peace. Even after her entrance into Carmel, fears and troubles continued to torment her.[9] She tells us: "At that time I suffered great interior trials of many kinds."[10] Only in 1891, after three years of religious life, is she "understood in a wonderful manner"[11] by Père Alexis. This religious assured her that the faults which troubled her "do not grieve God."[12] This was really the echo of her inmost thoughts and it "launched her in full sail upon the sea of confidence and love which attracted her so strongly but upon which she had not dared to venture."[13]

Guided by God from suffering to suffering, from reef to reef,

---

[8] S.S. p. 87; Ms. A, fol. 45 v°.
[9] Cf. S.S. p. 123; Ms. A, fol. 70 r°; Dep. of Mother Agnes; Sum. p. 13; Sum. p. 625.
[10] S.S. p. 138; Ms. A, fol. 80 v°.   [12] *Ibid.*
[11] *Ibid.*   [13] *Ibid.*

Thérèse abandons herself wholly to the way of confidence opened to her. From now on what will prevent her becoming the great saint she longs to be? "With love she not only advances; she flies."[14]

Nevertheless, everything does not become easy, everything does not change in her by the sole fact that she has confidence. A page of The Story of a Soul reveals the heart of the problem which then presents itself.

"You know, Mother, I have always desired to be a saint but, alas! I have always found, when comparing myself with the saints, that there is between them and me the same difference that there is between a mountain whose summit is lost in the heavens and an obscure grain of sand, trampled underfoot by passersby."[15]

An unexciting statement, only too true, which each one of us makes in his turn. Thérèse, however, is not discouraged nor does she exhaust herself in impossible efforts. She does not expect that the practice of virtues will make her a saint. Nor does she believe that grace can accomplish everything in her, without her: "Instead of becoming discouraged by such reflections, I said to myself: 'The good God would not inspire desires which could not be realized. . . . It is impossible for me to grow up so I must bear with myself just as I am with all my imperfections.' "[16] With faith and tenacity she strives to be a saint by being what she is: little, imperfect and without strength. Let us listen to her, rather: "I want to find a means of going to heaven — a little way, very straight, very short and entirely new. . . . I should also like to find a lift to carry me up to Jesus, for I am too little to climb the steep stairway of perfection."[17]

Her confidence is in Him who "gives no desires which He cannot satisfy."[18] Thérèse turns to Him and in Sacred Scripture reads these words of Eternal Wisdom: "Whosoever is a little one, let him come to me."[19] Her heart thrills with joy. The invitation is clear: God does not wait for very little ones to become great before showing them His attention; such as they are, He invites them to come to Him.

---

[14] Ibid.
[15] S.S. p. 151; Ms. C, fol. 2 v°.
[16] S.S. p. 151; Ms. C, fol. 2 v°.
[17] S.S. p. 152; Ms. C, fol. 2 v° and 3 r°.
[18] L. p. 290.
[19] S.S. p. 152; Ms. C, fol. 3 r°; Prov. 9:4.

"I therefore drew near to God, certain that I had discovered what I was seeking. But wanting to know what He would do for a little one who answered His invitation, I continued my search, and this is what I found: 'You shall be carried at the breasts, and upon the knees they shall caress you. As one whom the mother caresseth, so will I comfort you.' "[20]

Thérèse has found that not only can little ones attain perfection but that it is God Himself who takes all sorrow from them, who accomplishes everything through His sweetness and His mercy. "Oh, never have more tender, more melodious words delighted my soul. The lift to raise me up to Heaven is Thy arms, O Jesus!"[21]

Thus, for His little ones, God is All. Not only is He their sole end but He is also their way, their divine lift. They have only to offer no resistance but follow His movement.

Thérèse has experienced the divine action. She knows that, incapable of sanctifying herself, she must let God act in her; with confidence, she abandons herself to His operation. This is already a step in the spiritual life which too few souls accomplish with generosity.

But the saint's originality is greater than this. She has all the daring of a child who knows himself loved and, in addition, she possesses a subtle and disconcerting logic. She knows that God *can do everything* in her soul. Through her reading of Scripture she realizes that He *wills* to do everything in the souls of little ones. Therefore she decides not only to let God act but *to oblige Him to act* in her, for her and through her and to oblige Him to act unceasingly. How will she carry out such a plan?

1. *By remaining little.* Thérèse can neither do nor attain what she desires, but she knows that Jesus can. She straightforwardly declares that she *wants* to remain little forever and that she does not want ever to be able to form her own holiness — this, in order that God may accomplish it Himself.

"For that I do not need to grow," she says; "on the contrary, I must remain little; I must become even smaller."[22] "Even among the poor the child is given all he needs but as soon as he grows

[20] S.S. p. 152; Ms. C, fol. 3 r°; Isa. 66:12–13.
[21] S.S. p. 152; Ms. C, fol. 3 r°.   [22] S.S. p. 152; Ms. C, fol. 3 r°.

up, his father no longer wishes to support him and says, 'Go to work now; you are able to look after yourself.' It is to avoid hearing this that I have not wanted to grow up, feeling myself incapable of earning my living, the eternal life of heaven!"[23]

Thus she expects to oblige God to lower Himself to her nothingness. Only then in Thérèse's life does the experience of her weakness become her delight forever; she establishes herself truly, lovingly, in the "nothingness" of the creature. Her misery is her joy, her livelihood, and she uses it at each instant as a lure for divine Omnipotence.

Remaining little, Thérèse does not renounce her great ambitions for holiness. On the contrary! In this voluntary and joyous acceptance of her wretchedness she has found the unique means of realizing her infinite desires: having them fulfilled by the very One who placed them in her heart. Thus, in consenting to be imperfect and miserable that God alone may be, in her, her perfection, her strength and her holiness, Thérèse will attain, as she desires, "to the summit of the mountain of love";[24] she will arrive there even more quickly than by any other road. She truly discovered for herself and for us a little, a "very short"[25] way leading to the heart of God more quickly than all human stairways can. Such is the enviable lot of the very little ones. The great ones have a number of complicated means for arriving at perfection — or attempting to; the little ones have only one, but an infallible one: it is God alone.

2. *By offering herself to Love.* Thérèse, therefore, accepts her littleness and unceasingly presents it to God as a motive for Him to act in and through her. But she takes a second step: she offers herself to Merciful Love. Why? Because in the text of Isaias,[26] as throughout all the Gospel, she sees Love especially at work in little ones; Love stooping to little ones, ever surrounding them. She longs to surrender herself entirely to Love. In discovering her own secret Thérèse feels — and this explains her audacity — that she has discovered the secret of Jesus, His longing "to let the floods of infinite tenderness pent up in Him overflow"[27] into a multitude of

23 N.V. pp. 87–88.
24 S.S. p. 197; Ms. B, fol. 1 v°.
25 S.S. p. 152; Ms. C, fol. 2 v°.

26 Cf. Isa. 66:13.
27 Cf. Act of Oblation, L. p. 375; Ms. Appendix.

little souls, so poor in all human power that there is no barrier to the tide.

Seeing divine Charity burning to communicate Itself, and aware of the participation she may have in it, Thérèse's desire knows no bounds; she aspires to follow love at each moment and to receive its divine inflowing. Eager to live "an *act of perfect love*"[28] she begs God "ever to consume her."[29] She longs to be identified with Him: "I asked Jesus to draw me into the flames of His love, to unite me so intimately with Him that He will live and act in me."[30]

Thérèse would suppress nothing human — for that would be quietism — but she would have God take everything to Himself in love. When, at the evening of her life, Mother Agnes remarked that she must have had many struggles to attain the degree of perfection seen in her, Thérèse replied with indefinable emphasis: "Oh, it isn't that!"[31] In this single exclamation she summed up her whole secret and her spiritual ambition. Unquestionably, she made an effort in her life but it was one effort: that of remaining united to Jesus, of expecting everything from Him alone. In this single effort lies Thérèse's real strength, all her efficacy. It never bore directly on an obstacle but consisted in keeping fixed on Jesus alone a look full of confidence, as an invitation for Him to do His work in her. Instead of being troubled about her sanctity, instead of straining toward it, Thérèse has cast everything onto God. Her only care is to keep her heart ever open to receive Him. This "disposition of the heart,"[32] permits God Himself to take charge of the activity of His creature and to exceed her expectations by becoming her virtue and holiness. Because her secret has not deceived the little saint, "all her hopes," she affirms, "have been realized."[33]

We cannot do better than to turn to the Gospel with its positive words: love your heavenly Father, as very poor little children, to be sure, but very confident ones who care only to look at Him and always to please Him. That is sanctity stripped of the very human garb which too often disguises it; that is real holiness, beloved of God and accessible to all.

[28] *Ibid.*
[29] Cf. Act of Oblation, L. p. 375; Ms. C, fol. 36 r°.
[30] S.S. p. 193; Ms. C, fol. 36 r°.   [32] N.V. p. 78.
[31] N.V. p. 78.   [33] Cf. N.V. p. 139.

THÉRÈSE AND THE EUCHARIST

The spirit of childhood which characterizes Thérèse's spiritual progress is especially noticeable in her attitude toward the Eucharist. Certainly, like so many saints, Thérèse desires and passionately loves the Eucharist because the sacred Host is Christ, but her manner of receiving the Bread of Life and of living in It is that of the evangelical child. Moreover, in the measure that she discovers in the sacred Host the model of Christ's humility and the supreme pledge of His love, the more deeply she enters into the way of humility and confidence, until at last she longs to be identified with the sacred Host, to disappear in Jesus in total abandonment.

On the day of her First Communion Thérèse markedly experienced the love of Jesus. "For a long time Jesus and Thérèse had *looked* at and understood each other. . . . That day it was no longer a *look* but a *fusion*. They were no longer two; Thérèse had disappeared like a drop of water lost in the depths of the ocean. Jesus alone remained. He was the Master, the King. Had not Thérèse asked Him to take away the *liberty* which frightened her? She felt herself so weak and frail, that she wanted to be forever united to divine strength."[34]

The Eucharist is the gift of divine strength to the child who is conscious of his weakness, and the point of "fusion" where he who is nothing tends to lose himself in Him who is All. Thérèse lets herself be invaded by the plenitude of God; the following days, she repeats unceasingly: "It is now no longer I that live, but Christ lives in me."[35]

1. The attitude of Thérèse toward the Eucharist is permeated with this spirit of childhood as she prepares for Holy Communion, receives It, makes her thanksgiving or tells us what she expects from the sacrament.

Strengthened in divine love, Thérèse, in approaching the holy table, will, henceforth, think more of Jesus than of herself and her weakness. She is only fifteen when she explains to her cousin, Marie Guerin: "O my dear one, do you realize that Jesus is there in the

---

[34] S.S. p. 74; Ms. A, fol. 35 r°.
[35] S.S. p. 76; Ms. A, fol. 36 r°; Gal. 2:20.

tabernacle expressly for you, for you alone? He burns with the desire to come into your heart."[36] This is the essential point: Jesus has an immense desire to come to us:

> "I thirst to give myself to souls,
> But many hearts are languishing."[37]

Thérèse, moreover, knows well:

> "My soul to Jesus is more dear
> Than precious vases of gold."[38]

This is why she denounces a diabolical snare in the scruples of her cousin, who, after the least fault, did not dare to approach the holy table: "Do not listen to the devil, laugh at him, and go without fear to receive the Jesus of peace and love!"[39]

Thérèse receives Holy Communion, above all, "in order to give pleasure to Jesus,"[40] finding her joy in pure faith and not letting herself be stopped by aridity: "I can not say that I have often received consolations during my thanksgivings; that is probably the time that I have fewer. . . . I find that very natural since I have offered myself to Jesus, not as a person who wishes to receive His visit for my own consolation, but for the pleasure of Him Who gives Himself to me."[41]

If she considers her weakness, it is only to enter further on the path of humility and to redouble her confidence in love. One day God gives her a special light on her misery at the moment of reciting the *Confiteor* before Holy Communion: "I saw our Lord ready to give Himself to me, and that confession seemed to me a very necessary humiliation. . . . I felt myself to be like the publican, a great sinner, and God appeared so merciful. I found it so touching to address the heavenly court, to obtain through its intercession the forgiveness of my sins. . . . It was extraordinary to have had that experience at the *Confiteor*. I believe that it is the explanation of my present disposition: for I see myself so miserable. My confidence, however, is not in the least diminished because of that;

---

36 L. p. 107.
37 P. "The Angels of the Crib."
38 P. "My Desires Near the Tabernacle."

39 L. pp. 107–108.
40 S.S. p. 142.
41 S.S. p. 142; Ms. A, fol. 79 v°.

on the contrary. But the word miserable does not express what I should say, since I am rich with all the divine treasures. However, it is just that which makes me humble myself the more."[42]

Rather than remain at the level of her wretchedness, of which she is fully conscious, rather than try to justify herself, Thérèse lifts her gaze to Jesus: "Our God, the Guest of our heart . . . comes to us with the hope of finding a dwelling place, an empty tent, in the midst of the world's battlefield. He asks no more than that."[43]

Far from receiving Jesus without fervor, Thérèse puts aside her own merits to clothe herself with those of her mother: "Picturing my soul as waste land, I beg the Blessed Virgin to take away the rubbish which prevents its being *free*, and to erect a spacious pavilion worthy of *Heaven* and to beautify it with her own adornments. I next invite all the saints and the angels to make a grand concert. Then it seems to me that Jesus descends into my heart, and He is pleased to find Himself so well received and I, too, am pleased."[44] Thérèse has grasped how the Eucharist is thanksgiving, an enthusiastic recognition of the divine benefits: *Gratias agimus Domino Deo nostro* . . . God expects from His creature only the humble recognition of what she has received. This is the gift which rejoices Him more, for it exactly corresponds to God's own nature: the Love whose glory it is to communicate Itself.

Receiving Jesus "to give Him pleasure,"[45] Thérèse knows that at the same time she will receive from Him what is necessary for her in order to live; this is the value that, throughout her life, she will attach to Holy Communion. Mother Agnes of Jesus tells us: "After her First Communion, she longed for her Communion days, finding them too far apart."[46] At the time of her last illness she overcame extreme weakness amid trials and sufferings in order to receive Communion: "I do not find that it is too much to suffer to gain a Communion,"[47] she replies to a Sister who reproaches her conduct. To communicate is to receive divine strength:

[42] N.V. pp. 96–97.
[43] L. p. 231.
[44] S.S. p. 142; Ms. A, fol. 79 v° and fol. 80 r°.
[45] S.S. p. 142; cf. Ms. A, fol. 79 v°.
[46] Sum. p. 268.
[47] Sum. p. 300.

"My daily bread,
Jesus — 'tis Thou!"[48]

And to a novice (designated by the symbol of the forget-me-not) who wanted to deny herself Holy Communion because of an infidelity, Thérèse explains: "The forget-me-not need only unfold, or rather, uplift its petals for the Bread of Angels to come like a divine dew to strengthen it and give it all it lacks."[49]

Thérèse even expects a greater apostolic fruitfulness from her union with the Eucharistic Jesus than from her own works:

"Living Bread, Bread of Heaven, Divine Eucharist,
O touching Mystery produced by Love,
Come dwell within my heart, Jesus, my white Host . . .
Deign to unite me unto Thee, O holy and sacred Vine,
That my feeble branch may yield its fruit to Thee;
And I will offer Thee a gilded cluster . . .
This cluster of love of which the grapes are souls."[50]

For Thérèse the Eucharist is the sacrament of the missionary apostolate, the sacrament of the growth of the Church. Through it, by means of mutual love, the Christian community grows in sanctity and number. It fosters the reunion of the children of God scattered by sin.

2. Approaching the Eucharist as a child, the saint discovers more and more the mystery of humility which Jesus embraced through love and in which she longs to join Him. This aspect recurs constantly in her poems:

"My heaven is hidden in the little Host
Where Jesus, my Spouse, hides Himself through love."[51]

"Thou, the great God Whom the universe adores,
In me Thou liv'st, a prisoner night and day."[52]

She has Jesus speak:

"Yes, 'tis your heart which I desire,
To it I come to abase Myself."[53]

The host is the model of the spirit of evangelical childhood.

---

48 P. "Jesus, My Beloved, Remember Thou."
49 S.S. pp. 321–322.
50 P. "My Song of Today"; cf. Jn. 15:5.

51 P. "My Heaven."
52 P. "I Thirst for Love."
53 P. "Jesus at Bethany."

Therefore, when Thérèse composes a prayer to obtain humility she turns directly to the Eucharist:
"Now, it is in the Host that I see Thee complete Thy annihilation. What humility Thou hast, O divine King of Glory, to submit Thyself to all Thy priests, without any distinction between those who love Thee and those who, alas, are lukewarm or cold in Thy service. . . . O my Beloved, beneath the veil of the white Host, Thou dost appear to me meek and humble of heart. To teach me humility Thou canst not further abase Thyself; so I wish to respond to Thy love by putting myself in the lowest place."[54]

For Thérèse, humility, born from the acceptance of her weakness, has become an imitation of Jesus in the Eucharist.

> "Thou liv'st, for me, hidden in a host,
> For Thee I wish to hide myself, O Jesus.
> Lovers need solitude,
> A heart-to-heart which lasts night and day."[55]

3. By ever greater devotion to Jesus in the Eucharist Thérèse enters more fully into the way of spiritual childhood. That participation in the Eucharistic mystery brings her to the perfection of abandonment. Better still, after her First Communion, Thérèse finds in the Eucharist, the way of "losing herself" in Jesus:

> "I am Thy cherished spouse,
> Come, my Beloved, live in me.
> O come, Thy beauty hast ravished me,
> Deign *to transform me into Thee*."[56]

Such is the will of Jesus, to fill us with His plenitude:

> "He wishes to change you into Himself . . .
> Be His white and pure host."[57]

In the measure in which the creature consents to "lose herself" in God, she is completely possessed by Him; it is the way of littleness, fully embraced, with all the suffering that this total gift represents:

---

[54] S.S. p. 453.
[55] P. "To Live By Love"; cf. Col. 3:3.
[56] P. "My Desires Near the Tabernacle." (The italics are the author's.)
[57] P. "The Divine Little Beggar of Christmas."

"Jesus, O holy and sacred vine . . .
I am a gilded cluster
Who for Thee must disappear.
Under the winespress of suffering
I shall prove my love for Thee,
I desire no other joy
Than to immolate myself each day."[58]

Here Thérèse finds anew the great Eucharistic values. Here she seeks strength for the opening out of her soul. Here she attains union with God. For all of us today the Mass actually reproduces, in an unbloody manner, the sacrifice that Jesus realized in a bloody manner on Calvary. And Jesus comes to us in the sacrament in order to draw us unreservedly into His offering, so that each day our sacrifice may be lost in His. In Christ, in the Eucharist, our entire existence becomes God's, a continuous passage from the state of sin to the joy of divine intimacy.

Such a "disappearance" in Jesus is realized at each instant in abandonment. At the end of her life when Thérèse wants to live only in a complete resignation of her will and humbly, confidently surrender herself to the Father, she explicitly establishes a bond between the Eucharist and this attitude of soul:

"Abandonment alone delivers me
Into Thy arms, O Jesus!
It makes me live
On the bread of Thy elect . . .
My sweet sun of life . . .
'Tis Thy divine Host,
Small like me . . .
Of its celestial flame,
The luminous ray
Brings to birth in my soul
Perfect abandonment."[59]

Consequently, Thérèse does not separate the sacramental life from the theological life. She subordinates to the Eucharist the entire practice of the way of childhood, because It is essentially "the living Bread of Faith,"[60] the "Bread of exile,"[61] which alone

---

[58] P. "My Desires Near the Tabernacle."
[59] P. "Abandonment."
[60] P. "Jesus, My Beloved, Remember Thou."
[61] *Ibid.*

gives the strength to fight the good fight to the end and to attain heaven; so she concludes the poem on "Abandonment" (fruit of love):

> "I await in peace the glory
> Of the heavenly abode,
> For I find in the ciborium
> The sweet fruit of love."[62]

The Eucharistic Jesus comes "to dwell" with us solely in order to guide us toward the lasting city, "for here we have no permanent city, but we seek for the city that is to come."[63] As formerly a luminous presence guided the Hebrews toward the Promised Land, the Eucharist aids us, with Christ, "to pass out of this world to the Father."[64] It is our strength for the journey, the sacrament of our "passage." At the same time it is a foretaste of the Celestial Banquet, the sign of the new and eternal Alliance. The sacrament of hope, it even now radiates the peace and joy of final possession.

The childish images used by Thérèse, particularly in her poems, to express her tenderness toward the "Beloved," cannot mislead. Her devotion to the Eucharist is theological. "I sing simply what I want to believe,"[65] she says clearly about her poems; this is her reply to the common belief that she was filled with consolations. Her eyes see only the appearances but her heart discovers the supreme abasement of Jesus and the call to follow Him. The absence of sensible satisfaction is for her another way of giving Him more love.

> "My heaven is in the smile of this God Whom I adore . . .
> When He hides Himself to test my faith;
> To smile while waiting for His gaze once more,
> That is my heaven! . . ."[66]

Thérèse attaches herself only to the interests of Jesus, to whatever she knows in faith; she takes literally the words of Scripture and clings to them with her whole being.

Thus to communicate for the sole pleasure of Jesus is the manifestation of a noble and gratuitous charity, which does not hesitate

---

[62] P. "Abandonment."
[63] Hebr. 13:14.
[64] Jn. 13:1.

[65] S.S. p. 158; Ms. C, fol. 7 v°.
[66] P. "My Heaven."

to efface itself before the Beloved. Jesus is Thérèse's only thought; for Him alone does she hope; from Him alone does she await everything.

THÉRÈSE AND MARY

Thérèse is no less a child in her relations with the most Blessed Virgin than she is with God. But whereas she expects holiness from the heavenly Father, she entrusts all the details of her life to Mary.

Let us recall briefly the charming intimacy of the saint with her Mother; then let us see how this intimacy grew in the measure that Thérèse discovered in Mary the perfect and imitable model of evangelical childhood, in the measure that she abandoned herself to Mary's motherhood of grace until she became identified with the child of God par excellence, the Immaculate.

1. Thérèse has written little on the Blessed Virgin. We find a few scattered allusions in her poems and her letters, and Novissima Verba has preserved for us some revealing confidences; but it is in the long poem, "Why I Love Thee, O Mary,"[67] written several months before her death, that Thérèse endeavored to express all the wealth of her Marian experience. Sister Genevieve says, "I still hear her telling me that before dying she wanted to express all she thought about the Blessed Virgin."[68] To appreciate Thérèse's canticle, each verse ought to be accompanied by the engaging melody she chose.[69] It is her last song. As she reviews in spirit her life now ending in immolation, she sees one person in everything: Mary, "whom she lovingly called Mama."[70]

Thérèse's Marian life coincided with her religious consciousness. The little girl's love for Mary is innate, a supernatural instinct. She has known many trials: when she was four years old, the death of her mother; later, her "little mother"[71] Pauline's departure for Carmel; then her own strange illness. In all these trials her confidence in Mary had emerged strengthened, to remain throughout her life what it had been here, immediate and spontaneous.

---

[67] On the melody of "The Lament of the Cabin-Boy."
[68] M. p. 122.
[69] P. "Why I Love Thee, O Mary," on the melody of "The Lament of the Cabin-Boy."
[70] M. p. 122.   [71] N.V. p. 32.

Thérèse hopes for everything from her Mother, both for herself: "She does my commissions well!"[72] and for souls: "Thérèse confidently believed that all conversions could be obtained by the invocation of Mary."[73] She shares everything with her Mother. In all the details of her life Thérèse relies on her especially. "To ask something of the Blessed Virgin is not the same as to ask it of the good God. She knows well what to do with my little desires; and it is for her to decide whether to ask for them or not. . . . In the end it is for her not to force God to answer me, but to leave all to His will."[74]

Mary is her infirmarian and assists her in her sufferings. "During the night, being unable to do more, I asked the Blessed Virgin to take my head in her hands, so that I might be able to support it."[75] "I have suffered much, very much, but it is to the Blessed Virgin I make my complaint. . . ."[76] Is not Mary the refuge of the dying? "The Blessed Virgin held her dead Jesus, disfigured and blood-stained! This is very different from what you will see!"[77] No uncertainty can shake this child's confidence: "When we pray to the Blessed Virgin and she does not answer us, we ought to let her do what she pleases, without insisting, and not go on tormenting ourselves. . . ."[78] What mother's heart would not be disarmed by confessions like this: "Last evening I asked the Blessed Virgin not to let me cough any more so that Sister Genevieve might be able to sleep but I added: If you do not do this, I shall love you all the more!"[79]

In the most cruel temptations, in the night of the soul when even Jesus will be hidden from her, Thérèse can still look at Mary. During her last illness when the statue of Mary was placed near her bed, "Thérèse's gaze was constantly turned toward her. . . ."[80]

Let us not see this attachment in a bad light or as purely sentimental. In her own way, with imagery, directness and theological truth, Thérèse voices the reason for her confidence. She knows that only in Jesus are we children of Mary:

72 N.V. p. 20.   77 N.V. p. 63.
73 M. p. 122.   78 N.V. p. 112.
74 N.V. p. 15.   79 N.V. p. 99.
75 N.V. p. 102.   80 M. p. 121.
76 N.V. p. 123.

"Of the countless numbers of His sinful brethren,
We must call Him: *Jesus thy firstborn*."[81]

and that in heaven Mary "remains our support."[82] The immediate consequence: "The treasure of the mother belongs to the child";[83] calmly Thérèse takes possession of it, with a freedom and naturalness that rejoices her mother. Since we are children, let us remain children to the end. This is the saint's Marian thought; she consciously co-operates with the hidden design of the Father, who has revealed it to His little ones:

"The Lord knows thy boundless tenderness;
He knows the secrets of thy maternal heart."[84]

From these thousand attentions and kindnesses a true intimacy develops between the Virgin and Thérèse. The images that the saint affectionately uses to describe Mary are those of a very little girl: she sees herself in Mary's arms, clasped to her heart beneath her veil or singing on her knees. This touching realism constantly rejuvenates her love. But beyond all the images, what filial abandonment, what intimacy at every moment!

"To believe myself thy child is not difficult!"[85]

Close to her mother whose "maternal glance banishes all her fears," Thérèse understands the loving heart of God, very simply she responds; she lives with Mary as she lives with God: in the trust of a child. The "little way" is already there in germ. Mary awakens the soul to the values of childhood. "It is to recognize our nothingness . . . to await everything from God . . . to be disturbed about nothing . . . and not to be set on gaining our fortune . . . always to remain little, having no other occupation than that of gathering the flowers of love . . . not to attribute to ourselves the virtues we practice . . . not to be discouraged over our faults."[86] In Thérèse's eyes all this constitutes spiritual childhood, the only proper attitude toward a mother. The greater this intimacy, the

[81] P. "Why I Love Thee, O Mary."
[82] *Ibid*. Cf. Memorare.
[83] P. "Why I Love Thee, O Mary."
[84] *Ibid*.
[85] P. "Why I Love Thee, O Mary."
[86] N.V. pp. 87–88.

deeper Thérèse will enter into the spirit of the Beatitudes; the more she surrenders to the Virgin, the more does she act as the daughter of God, for living fully abandoned to Mary, she enters more fully into the heart of the Father.

2. Intimacy nourishes itself on a continual conversation, wherein love seeks to know and to communicate. Now trials multiply for Thérèse; in the measure in which she is consumed, solitude becomes the more oppressive. Thérèse's affection for her "Mama"[87] and her fondness for endearing expressions need not mislead us; though her heart remains a child's heart, the realities confronting her are those of an adult and a mystic. More than ever she feels the need of a real mother, to walk with her "on the strange shore,"[88] for "this is exile indeed in all its rigor."[89]

> "That a child may cherish his Mother
> She must weep with him . . ."[90]

"In pondering her life written in the Gospels,"[91] Thérèse finds our Lady as gentle and sorrowful as she, but with a surpassing peace:

> "I see thee mortal and suffering like me . . .
> . . . I dare to look at and to come near to thee . . ."[92]

"I understood that she had suffered not only in soul but also in body. She suffered much on her journeys from cold, heat and fatigue. . . . She fasted many times. . . . Yes, she knows what it is to suffer."[93]

She loves Mary's simplicity very much.[94] "How I should have loved to be a priest, that I might preach about the Virgin Mary! . . . First, I should have shown how little is known of her life. It is not good to say things about her that are improbable, or that we do not know. . . . For a sermon on the Blessed Virgin to bear fruit, it must show her real life, as the Gospel sets it before us, and not her supposed life."[95] Certainly, Thérèse blessed the Almighty for

---

[87] M. p. 122.
[88] P. "Why I Love Thee, O Mary."
[89] Ibid.
[90] Ibid.
[91] Ibid.

[92] Ibid.
[93] N.V. p. 104.
[94] N.V. Cf. pp. 104–105.
[95] N.V. pp. 109–110.

having done great things in Mary;[96] "It is good to speak of her prerogatives but we must not stop there. We must make her loved."[97] Thérèse wants her mother near us, that we may love her and make her loved; Nazareth fascinates her:

"I know that at Nazareth, O Virgin full of grace,
Thou liv'st very poorly desiring nothing;
No raptures, nor miracles, nor ecstacies . . ."[98]

Nothing but the silent, loving accomplishment of daily duty. Because Jesus has willed His mother to "be the example of the soul who seeks Him in the night of faith,"[99] and that she "has known the submission of the night, the anguish of heart."[100]

St. Thérèse has so stressed Mary's evangelical humility and simplicity because in her mother she finds a hidden soul living the act of abandonment to God's will. Having lived perfection, Mary becomes the personification of spiritual childhood; she is the handmaid. . . . In this sense the "little way" was the Immaculate's discovery before being Thérèse's; the saint's genius was understanding our need of a mother through whom we become true children of God and discovering in Mary all the requirements of abandonment.

3. "Instead of presenting the Blessed Virgin as all but inaccessible, we should show her as imitable; she practised the hidden virtues and lived by faith just as we must do. . . ."[101]

"We know the Blessed Virgin is Queen of Heaven and earth but she is more mother than queen."[102] What sureness of doctrine in Thérèse's words!

Intimacy with her has revealed to Thérèse Mary's love, her contemplation, her ineffable beauty; but by living ever under her influence Thérèse experiences the power of her Queen and draws from her motherhood of grace the strength to imitate her unto heroism.

Faithful to her set purpose of childhood, Thérèse clings to her mother: "I wish to live with thee, to follow thee each day."[103]

---

[96] P. "Why I Love Thee, O Mary."
[97] N.V. p. 111.
[98] P. "Why I Love Thee, O Mary."
[99] Ibid.
[100] P. "Why I Love Thee, O Mary."
[101] N.V. p. 110.
[102] N.V. p. 111.
[103] P. "Why I Love Thee, O Mary."

"Without delay and without reasoning,"[104] Thérèse will imitate Mary's obedience, her humility which ravishes God and draws the Blessed Trinity into her heart, and her silence in the presence of Joseph's anguish:

> "When the good Saint Joseph knew not the miracle. . . .
> Thou didst let him weep near the tabernacle
> Which veils the divine beauty of the Lord."[105]

This is attractive description; but the drama of it has been felt — and lived — by Thérèse. The mystery of the ways of God!

Mary gently draws her toward the interior life: all is obscured which is not God. Mary's presence, far from distracting the child, deepens her loving solitude and silence. There, close to the "Queen of her heart,"[106] Thérèse enjoys the peace of the pure of heart who see God:

> ". . . in poverty thy heart remains joyous;
> For is not Jesus the most beautiful fatherland?
> What matters exile? . . . thou possesseth the heavens!"[107]

Above all, Thérèse will learn from the Immaculate the greatness of littleness. But

> ". . . That I may always shelter thee
> Beneath my veil near Jesus,
> Thou must remain little.
> . . . And if someone repeats
> That thy works do not show:
> 'I love very much,' you can say,
> 'That is my labor here below.' "[108]

To love in obscurity, to welcome the interior light is the Marian secret illuminating Thérèse's "little way." Has she not rediscovered in it the fundamental attitude of "the poor ones of Yahweh," who walk sorrowfully through the Old Testament, and whose prayer rises in a crescendo, up to the *Magnificat* of the Virgin?

Mary sings, "He has regarded the lowliness of His handmaid," and Thérèse, dying, echoes her: "Yes, I have understood humility

104 *Ibid.*
105 *Ibid.*
106 *Ibid.*
107 *Ibid.*
108 P. "The Queen of Heaven to Her Little Mary" (composed for a postulant).

of heart."[109] She has a presentiment that multitudes will follow her on this Marian way:

> "The number of little ones is very great on earth,
> They can, without trembling, lift their eyes to thee."[110]

Our saint is not content with this gaze. Sharing the intuition of great Marian mystics, she seems to have had a sort of identification with Our Lady,

> "Like thee I possess in me the All-Powerful. . . .
> Thy virtues, thy love, are they not mine? . . ."[111]

to such an extent that Jesus Himself might nearly be mistaken:

> "So when into my heart the white Host descends,
> Jesus, my sweet Savior, thinketh to rest in thee!"[112]

And is not the great mystical grace of July, 1889, linked to the Marian life of Thérèse?

> "It was as if a veil had been thrown for me over all the things of earth . . . I seemed to be entirely hidden beneath the Blessed Virgin's veil . . . I performed my actions as though I performed them not; it was as if I were acting in a borrowed body."[113]

On her bed of illness Thérèse sings, "With thee I have suffered."[114] Step by step with Jesus and Mary she approaches Calvary by way of abandonment. For love burns away everything that would make the soul unacceptable in the sight of God. But what does it matter!

> "Everything that He has given me, Jesus can take again;
> Tell Him never to inconvenience Himself for me. . . ."[115]

The Father who sees in secret took Thérèse at her word; it pleased Him to bruise her in infirmity.[116] Standing close to her "disconsolate mother," Thérèse directs her own life. From the high place of suffering, she can better grasp the fullness of God's plan and the mysterious inconsistencies of His love: "It is good to suffer on earth."[117] From now on she knows what it costs to love mankind. Her way has not deceived her; in the supernatural world in which she has developed since childhood, Thérèse sought no other strength

---

109 N.V. p. 138.
110 P. "Why I Love Thee, O Mary."   114 P. "Why I Love Thee, O Mary."
111 Ibid.   115 Ibid.
112 Ibid.   116 Cf. Isa. 53:10.
113 N.V. p. 42.   117 P. "Why I Love Thee, O Mary."

than self-effacement, no other joy than poverty, no other greatness than abandonment.

In Mary she has found a Queen and Patroness, a model so deeply human that she is always accessible. The life of Mary, the heart of Mary, are for her a living translation of the Gospel, the direct way of abandonment. But still more than the Queen Beauty, the Virgin is for Thérèse the mother who gives life and educates. The Story of a Soul is but the story of Mary's tenderness.[118]

Our Lady has gently led her child on a narrowing path, teaching her to live the joyful and sorrowful mysteries in darkness.

Glory? Thérèse feels that it is very near: "All is accomplished! It is love alone that counts."[119] And love will receive her. Even now the Father's inexpressible goodness shines more sweetly on the face of the Immaculate:

> "Thou who didst come to smile on me in life's morning,
> Come smile once more . . . Mother, 'tis evening!"[120]

2. The Secret of Thérèse in Her Relations With the Novices

In 1893, when Thérèse first began her duty as a teacher, her personal way was not as clear as it would be in the year of her death. With her new obligations demanding still greater vigilance, she is compelled to share her spiritual discoveries as soon as possible. Thérèse promptly puts into practice her fundamental intuitions. She neglects nothing she can do, but knowing her own helplessness, she awaits from God alone the strength to accomplish what she must do. She wants Him to work through her in souls.

Thérèse takes responsibility seriously. Conscious of the importance of this mission, she undertakes it gravely, like "a little paintbrush which Jesus has chosen to paint His likeness in souls."[121] This disposition is shown in another confidence of the saint. At this time Mother Agnes suggests that she be a spiritual sister to a future missionary. She brings the same fidelity to that. "Because I understood the obligations that I was taking upon myself, I set to work to redouble my fervor."[122] Her vigilance is extreme: "Since

---

[118] Cf. Ms. C, fol. 1 r°.
[119] N.V. p. 135.
[120] P. "Why I Love Thee, O Mary."

[121] S.S. p. 173; Ms. C, fol. 20 r°.
[122] S.S. p. 189; Ms. C, fol. 32 r°.

I placed myself in the arms of Jesus, I have been like a watchman on the look-out for the enemy, from the highest turret of a fortified castle. Nothing escapes me. . . . Never shall I imitate the hireling, who, seeing the wolf coming, leaves the sheep and flees. I am ready to give my life for them (my lambs)."[123]

The young Mistress gives herself unreservedly to her duties, and so conscientiously that her novices find her "severe."[124] But she acts in their interest, although it costs much to her nature. "Formerly, when I saw a Sister doing something which displeased me and which seemed irregular, I would say to myself: 'Oh! How good it would be if I could tell her what I think, show her that she is wrong.' Since it has become my duty to find fault, I assure you, Mother, that my opinion has changed. Now, when I see a Sister doing something which seems imperfect, I heave a sigh of relief and say to myself: 'What a blessing! It is not a novice and I am not obliged to correct her.'"[125]

This obligation to correct her Sisters is so painful to her, that she finds the prophet Jonas quite excusable when he fled before the face of the Lord rather than announce the ruin of Ninive.[126] Nonetheless, Thérèse's zeal is unflagging. "More than once it has been said to me: 'If you wish to obtain something from me, you must treat me with gentleness; you will gain nothing by being severe.' But I know that no one is a good judge in his own case."[127]

The *Conseils et Souvenirs* show her unceasingly watchful. She scolds the novice who complains of being weary; the one who wants to seek consolations near our Lord; the one who congratulates herself for an act of virtue; the one who saunters on her way to the laundry.[128] She teaches her Sisters not to give themselves up too much to what they do, not to fret about their occupations, but always to act with detachment of spirit.

At other times she consoles and encourages. She shows how to accept humiliation, how to profit from distractions, how to keep

---

[123] S.S. pp. 176–177; Ms. C, fol. 23 r° and v°.
[124] S.S. p. 177; Ms. C, fol. 23 r°.
[125] S.S. p. 182; Ms. C, fol. 27 v°.
[126] S.S. p. 176; Ms. C, fol. 23 r°.
[127] S.S. p. 178; Ms. C, fol. 23 v° and 24 r°.
[128] Cf. S.S. p. 308.

modesty of the eyes in the refectory. She composes a prayer of petition to ask for a certain grace. She writes notes which reveal the tenderness of her heart and her psychological and spiritual insight. Before she has finished reading it, she lends a book that might do good to a soul. She makes her young Sisters profit from all her interior lights.[129]

This simple sketch of Thérèse at work is sufficient for us not to imagine her lost in a false contemplation or lonely reverie. At each moment the love of God places her at the service of her Sisters in a very practical and concrete manner. She acts without disorder or eagerness, with strength and peace. Not for a moment is she anxious or tense; she does not depart from her calm, her contemplation. Confronted by a novice's panic, she is perfect mistress of herself; in grave danger of being burned alive because of another's imprudence, she remains calm and confident, silently offering herself to God.[130]

Thérèse has no illusions about the meaning and scope of her action. She no longer needs to experience her own helplessness; she has already more than gauged it in the work of her sanctification. Incapable of changing herself, she feels more incapable of reforming others. To her own helplessness are added the helplessness of her Sisters and their freedom. Instinctively Thérèse is aware of her limitations. "When I entered the sanctuary of souls, I saw at once that the task was beyond my strength."[131]

"In the abstract," she writes, "it seems easy to do good to souls, to make them love God more and to mold them to one's views and personal thoughts. But in reality it is not so. We soon learn that without God's help it is as impossible to do good to them, as it is to make the sun shine in the night."[132]

Thérèse is aware that in entrusting the Sisters to her, God has given her a place in His wholly supernatural work of the formation and sanctification of souls. She clearly understands that she can and must be only an instrument — but not to the point of being passive — and that she must be pliable and docile under divine

---

[129] Doc.
[130] M. p. 200.

[131] S.S. p. 175; Ms. C, fol. 22 r°.
[132] S.S. p. 176; Ms. C, fol. 22 v°.

direction. Then without the slightest hesitation Thérèse makes use of her discovery and rushes into her "lift."[133]

"I placed myself in the arms of the good God like a little child," she writes, "and I said to Him: 'Lord, I am too little to feed Your children but if, through me, You wish to give them what is suitable, fill my hand, and without leaving Your arms or turning my head, I shall give Your treasures to the soul who comes to me asking for food.' "[134] It is very easy to separate reality from the images expressing it. As Mistress of Novices, Thérèse uses the same devices for them as for her own sanctification: she aims only to unite herself to God in a total acceptance of her helplessness, to remain little and surrendered to love that God may be compelled to act in souls.

"Since I understood that it was impossible to do anything of myself, the task which you had given me seemed no longer difficult. I sensed that the one thing necessary was to unite myself more and more to Jesus, and that the rest would be given to me in addition. My hope has never been ill-founded: the good God was pleased to fill my hand each time I have needed sustenance for the souls of my Sisters."[135]

As she remains in the arms of God, Thérèse's sole desire is to give nothing but His graces to her novices; to give fully what she receives from Him, without distorting or wasting it. To fulfill this ideal she knows she must be lost in Jesus.

Although her care is to unite herself interiorly with God,[136] she does not intend to exclude all personal and direct action. Not for a moment does Thérèse separate divine action from human means. She uses means in absolute dependence upon God when He obviously wishes to use her to give Himself to souls. Therein lies the rectitude of her conduct. She has found the perfect balance between an angelism which could do without everything human, expecting heaven to offer novices already formed, and an activism which would cut itself off from the supernatural, placing all its trust in secondary causes, forgetful of the First Cause.

---

[133] S.S. p. 152; Ms. C, fol. 3 r°.   [135] S.S. p. 176; Ms. C, fol. 22 v°.

[134] S.S. p. 175; Ms. C, fol. 22 r° and v°.   [136] Cf. S.S. p. 176.

Having become, by the will of God, the first companion of the novices, Thérèse has a very real duty to fulfill toward her young Sisters. She does not think that God will do all without her; but she believes that, having chosen her despite, or rather, because of her littleness, He will generously give her the lights and the graces necessary to these souls. Therefore, she wants to obtain them by a daily increase in her own fidelity and pliability, so as to channel them to the novices.

In a practical way, what must she do? Nothing more, as she admits, than remain in habitual union with Jesus,[137] saying nothing, undertaking nothing, without having had recourse to Him, without having invoked the Blessed Virgin. "When she was asked a question," testifies a novice, "she always reflected a moment before replying."[138] Then, whether she felt herself inspired or not, she believed she had received divine guidance. Her dependence on God plunged her into the most profound humility. "The paintbrush could not boast of the masterpiece it had helped to produce, for it knows that artists are never at a loss; they toy with difficulties and, to amuse themselves, sometimes use the weakest and most defective instruments."[139]

The certainty that God gave her what she distributed to souls allows her in this regard a complete decisiveness. "I shall give Your treasures to the soul who comes to me asking for food. If she finds it to her liking," she says, "I shall know that it is not to me she owes it but to You; if she complains and finds bitter what I offer her, my peace will not be disturbed; I shall try to convince her that this food comes from You and I shall take care to give her no other."[140] This firmness is as necessary for a teacher as is humility; Thérèse herself stresses that the fruitfulness of her work with souls and her own peace of mind depend upon it.

Nevertheless, if God accomplishes a part of His work through the Mistress of Novices, she does not forget that there is another more secret and more important work, and that He can perfectly accomplish it without an intermediary. She does not think herself

[137] Cf. S.S. p. 176; Ms. C, fol. 22 v°.
[138] Sum., Extract from the Dep. of Sr. Marie of the Trinity.
[139] S.S. p. 173; Ms. C, fol. 20.
[140] S.S. pp. 175–176; Ms. C, fol. 22 v°.

necessary. When she feels the Master's nearness, she knows how to efface herself and to pray for souls, asking Jesus to work directly in them. To a novice she said: "The bell is ringing for prayer. I do not have time to console you; besides, I see clearly that I could not do so; for the time being God wishes you to suffer alone."[141] She does not shed her responsibility with this refusal; she prays for her little Sister, "asking our Lord to console her, to transform her soul and to let her see the value of suffering";[142] immediately her prayer is answered.

Later, during Thérèse's last illness, a similar incident occurred. The same novice, again transformed interiorly by God at the prayer of her Mistress, came to her to say: "Don't worry about me any more for I no longer feel sad. I feel that you are praying for me and your sufferings are gaining many graces for me." "Oh! What consolation you give me," Thérèse answered. "How good Jesus is to hear my prayers for you."[143]

Thérèse's secret was to persevere in her delicate task, never to consider it as a human and personal work; to refuse to let it become a preoccupation; to use it, on the contrary, to cling more closely to God. She wanted to perform all her duties with no other care than love. Thérèse had the heroism to conquer all natural anxiety, interior or exterior; she made her task the concern of Jesus. She never tried to solve the thousand daily difficulties on only the human level; keeping in contact with God, she saw Him accomplish all things through her and in her stead.

Strong in this experience and sure of the efficacy of her method, Thérèse could affirm several days before her death: "It is possible to remain little even in the most responsible offices, even throughout a long life. If I should die at eighty, if I had been in many monasteries and charged with numerous responsibilities, I should have remained as little as I am today."[144]

It is so true that every soul of good will, no matter what his toil and misery may be, can find in Jesus his way, his truth, and his life. The love of Jesus, when it has once captured a heart,

---

[141] S.S. p. 318.
[142] S.S. p. 319.
[143] Circ. p. 42.
[144] N.V. p. 132.

cannot lie dormant in it like an abstract and remote idea. It becomes a daily reality, a "fountain of water, springing up unto life everlasting."[145]

In her task of spiritual direction, Thérèse relies, therefore, on the desire for God which she finds in the souls of her novices. She works to free, to strengthen and fully to satisfy this desire while bringing it to its goal. We shall now consider this intuition, which gives the saint's teaching all its significance.

---

[145] Jn. 4:14.

The Teaching

The first objective of Thérèse, that of purifying her Sisters' thirst for God, is to convince them that "all that is not God is nothing."[1] Her second aim is to give their spiritual life the firm foundation of faith in Love. Lastly, to bring about the perfect fulfillment of their desire, she teaches them to surrender themselves to Love at every moment.

Does not the Gospel follow the same order? It is impossible to overemphasize the fact that Thérèse found in the Gospel the source of her "little way."

"Make ready the way of the Lord, make straight his paths,"[2] proclaims John the Baptist as he inaugurates the divine work.

"Believe . . . in me,"[3] Christ asks throughout His life; that is to say, believe in God's great love made manifest in Me.

"Abide in my love,"[4] is His supreme recommendation to the faithful disciples surrounding Him on the eve of His death.

Likewise, Thérèse depends, not by turns but simultaneously (for life does not divide itself into parts), on what may be called the three established principles in her teaching: renunciation through love, faith in Love and surrender to Love. By these three means she guides souls from their entrance into God's way to their full spiritual stature.

---

[1] Cf. L. p. 113.
[2] Lk. 3:4.

[3] Jn. 14:1.
[4] Jn. 15:9.

CHAPTER IV

The Requirements of Evangelical Childhood

1. The Desire for God

VARYING in age and opportunities, in detachment and devotion to prayer, souls who approach the religious life do so, if the call is authentic, with an ardent desire for God. This desire is the best indication of a true vocation; it is about the only valuable element that a novice brings to Religion and, lacking this, all the rest is of little worth.

This aspiration strives for a loving union with God in the case of a contemplative vocation, toward a loving service of God in the vocation to the active life. But under either form this desire is indispensable. For the dynamism of grace, in its essence, is identical in all the baptized. Every Christian is a son walking toward the Father; every baptized soul tends to union with Christ the Spouse.

The religious vocation is only a call from God which makes this desire for Him so moving and so absolute that everything yields to it. In response to His choice God asks the soul to give free course to the deep movement which is born of Him and carries her toward Him. To depend upon this desire for God is to depend upon God Himself. St. Catherine of Siena taught that only desire in us is capable of attaining to God because it alone can expand to the infinite. By her striking example Thérèse has rendered illustrious this doctrine, so secure and so often forgotten. With her, desire is of special importance. In her work with souls, just as in her own life, she fearlessly relies on it. She says: "The good God never gives desires that He cannot fulfill."[1] She does

[1] L. p. 290.

not let her ardent thirst for love be extinguished by a timorous confessor who judged it rash. "God made me desire what He wished to give me," she declares.[2]

When she was only fourteen Thérèse had an experience in teaching which fully revealed this to her and enlightened her on the importance of desire. Two children had been entrusted to her care for a few days. When she wished to secure good behavior "from her two little girls . . . she spoke to them of eternal rewards." So effective was this method of winning them that the saint exclaims: "Holy Baptism must implant the theological virtues very deeply in the soul, because even in early childhood they are observable, bearing fruit in sacrifices accepted in the hope of heavenly reward."[3]

At that time Thérèse was dealing only with children. When she has adults called to the perfection of love, she will not need to change her method. As she formerly depended on the desire of heavenly recompense, she depends now, with still more strength and reason, on the desire for God who gives Himself as reward. She takes her novices, as she took Jesus, "by the heart,"[4] but, if one can say it, by the "theological heart." She adds, clearly showing that she considers this direction essential: "Oh, how many souls would arrive at sanctity if they were well directed."[5]

In the beginning of religious life the novice's desire for God is not yet strong enough nor pure enough. She has just left the world and may yet remain there by secret attachment. Moreover, she risks becoming bogged down in the very practices of the observance and the spiritual life. The first work of the Mistress must be to purify the soul and to free this desire from all that can stifle it, so that it alone may motivate all her actions.

To accomplish this, Thérèse untiringly places before her young Sisters the reality of God and the nothingness of the creature, asking them not to stop on the way but to choose resolutely between the All and the nothing. "It is only Jesus Who IS," she repeats; "all the rest is nothing."[6]

2 S.S. p. 187; Ms. C, fol. 31 r°.
3 S.S. p. 98; Ms. A, fol. 52 v°.
4 Cf. S.S. pp. 309–310; "One must take Jesus by the heart; that is His weak point."
5 S.S. p. 99; Ms. A, fol. 53 r°.   6 L. p. 113.

This absolute primacy of God is the foundation of her spirituality. The soul's experimental consciousness of this primacy, the sense of the absolute and the thirst for simplicity flowing from it, constitute the indispensable elements of a Carmelite vocation.

If God in His watchful Providence wishes to universalize the message of Thérèse, which is rooted in Carmelite spirituality, may it not be that it corresponds to the needs of this age and that it echoes the strong intuition God gives souls of the absolute reality of His being of love? The daily experience of those who deal with the souls of the young seems to indicate this. Modern youth has an insatiable longing for that which passes but, at the same time, a painful nostalgia for something else. In the better gifted there is a remarkable ability to go straight to the end of all, an incoercible need to risk all.

But they also need to experiment, in order to believe and, above all, in order to give themselves. Our Lord hesitates no more than He did twenty centuries ago to deliver them from their need. So it is that we may find novices with undeniable faults yet filled with equally undeniable graces. "What . . . our hands have handled: of the Word of Life,"[7] they can say in their turn with the Apostle John. And, despite all their miseries, they are carried away by desire and capable of leaving all things for Him who draws them.

2. Liberty of Soul

"The Lord is the spirit; and where the Spirit of the Lord is, there is freedom."[8]

This truth, so dear to the saint, underlies the greatest part of the instructions collected by her novices. Liberty of soul and renunciation are, as a matter of fact, the two principal requirements that free us from our own tendencies; and they are the two important points in the teaching of Thérèse. Now, what is the basic principle of liberty of soul and renunciation which makes them complementary, if not this: All that is not Jesus is nothing and must be set aside to give place to Jesus alone.[9]

Gently but with untiring perseverance, the Mistress removes everything that may impede progress. "That is not God," she says

---

[7] 1 Jn. 1:1. [8] 2 Cor. 3:17. [9] Cf. L. p. 113.

when she sees a soul anxious about something; that is not the
way to go about it, when she encounters a too lively and too natural
endeavor; and always: we must look at God, desire Him, and let
Him work in us.

But how difficult it often is to make souls understand the nature
of this spiritual liberty, despite their profound need of it. What
prudence is necessary to teach them to distinguish it from its
counterfeit, which is laxity; what firmness is required to make them
overcome themselves!

The saint vehemently desired this interior renunciation, this
liberty of spirit, for her novices, for these create the environment
in which the true desire for God can freely flourish. She has experienced how necessary they are. To follow the way that God
traced for her, Thérèse had to free herself from most of her early
ideas, as well as from many of the pious practices in use around
her, which were not part of the Rule. Once she had thought them
good for her, but the day comes when she has to acknowledge
that they are not the means for her advancement in grace. She
knows under what conditions of humility, obedience, and fidelity
this liberty of spirit is attained; she steadfastly maintains her novices
there. Despite the courage that this liberation demands, she tire-
lessly strives to foster it in them. She knows its fruitfulness.

Thérèse accepts nothing for her Sisters that will needlessly constrain, fatigue, or impede their souls. She wants them to come to
the pure desire of God, the simple gaze on Him. "For simple
souls," she lays down the principle, "complicated methods are
unnecessary."[10] She eliminates anything savoring of anxiety or con-
tention, whether it concerns union with God, prayer, the pursuit
of perfection or mortification.

Thérèse always shows forth God and makes souls run to Him
without letting them stop at the means: God alone is the end,
the All. The means have value and importance only in the measure
that they are willed by Him. When a novice laments her inattention in explicitly directing her will to God and her inability to speak
to Him as she would wish, Thérèse reassures her:

"This direction of the will is not necessary for a soul wholly

[10] S.S. p. 190; Ms. C, fol. 33 v°.

given to our Lord. Doubtless, it is good to recollect one's spirit, but sweetly because constraint does not glorify the good God. He understands all the beautiful thoughts and expressions of love that we should like to offer Him, and He is content with our desires. Is He not our Father and are we not His little children?"[11]

Nor does she complicate prayer. For Thérèse prayer is "an office of love";[12] "it is something great and supernatural, dilating the soul and uniting it to Jesus."[13] Reduced to essentials, prayer is simple because everything can become love.

When a novice complains of her distractions, the Mistress explains how she can profit from them by praying for the persons who cause the distractions. When another is troubled because of the wanderings of her imagination, Thérèse replies: "I accept everything for the love of the good God, even extravagant thoughts that come to my mind and trouble me."[14] The saint reserves the same freedom for prayers asked for a special intention: "I cannot constrain myself to say: 'My God, this is for the Church; my God, this is for France,' etc. . . . God knows what to do with my merits. I have given everything to Him just to give Him pleasure. It would weary my mind to be saying to Him at each instant: 'Give this to Peter, that to Paul.' Whenever one of the Sisters asks this of me I do it at once and then I think no more about it."[15]

Liberty of the soul in prayer, liberty in the pursuit of perfection. Thérèse wishes to eliminate any narrow conceptions of good. One day Mother Agnes wanted her opinion on various practices of devotion or of perfection recommended by spiritual authors, practices which have discouraged souls. Thérèse answered: "With the exception of the Gospel, I find nothing much in books any more. This book is sufficient for me. I listen with delight to the words of Jesus telling me what I have to do: 'Learn from me, for I am meek and humble of heart.'[16] Those words give me peace."[17]

Thérèse always opposed practices or, more precisely, the notion that sanctity consists in a given practice, in the possession of a certain virtue, sought without detachment; for then it is to these

---

[11] M. p. 51.
[12] Ms. B, fol. 5 r°.
[13] S.S. p. 180; Ms. C, fol. 25 r° and v°.
[14] N.V. p. 16.

[15] N.V. p. 81.
[16] Mt. 11:29.
[17] N.V. p. 3.

things that the soul attaches itself and not to God. Perhaps without even being aware of it, she is greatly constrained in her progress toward Him who alone is necessary. Her love for Jesus, which is the only truly effective means of reaching Him, is stifled.

Even in mortification the Mistress teaches that it is necessary to maintain holy liberty. She was told of a priest who suffered from a violent itching without ever trying to relieve it.

"Oh," the humble Thérèse exclaimed, "all mortification is praiseworthy and meritorious when practiced in the belief that God asks it of us. If one is mistaken in the action, He accepts our good intention; but I could never bind myself that way and preoccupy myself so. I have practiced virtue on an entirely different scale according to this advice of our Holy Mother, St. Teresa of Avila: 'The Lord does not dwell, as we imagine, upon a multitude of trivial things; the soul must not be constrained in any way.' "[18]

To everything that confines the heart or preoccupies the spirit Thérèse prefers the freedom of a pure gaze which is directed toward God.

The saint is not in the least concerned (need one say it?) about giving the novices a false freedom or claiming it for herself. Of two things she would never choose the less perfect or the more pleasant. It is a question of an authentic spiritual liberty, a liberty according to the Spirit, of which the young Mistress herself gives this beautiful definition: "Seeing that all have followed the movement of the Holy Spirit and the Lord has said, 'say to the just man that it is well,' then all is well when we seek only the will of Jesus."[19] What is the will of God except to establish between His creature and Himself a lasting intercourse, a real exchange of love? Therefore, Thérèse would establish and maintain souls in an interior state of simplicity and poverty. In it they could follow the divine attraction without any hindrance and provide good ground for the desire which God has placed in them as a precious seed. It may be said, then, that Thérèse thus procures from God the liberty in guiding her novices and acting in them, with nothing human binding them to anything but Him. The Mistress respects God and the work of His loving wisdom, to the point of wishing souls

18 E. p. 173.   19 S.S. p. 151; Ms. C, fol. 2 v°.

not to be concerned with it: "You do not need to understand what God does in you," she says, "you are too little."[20] The quoted texts prove that we must not misunderstand Thérèse's true sense of fidelity in little things. It does not consist in too many practices, in devotions which imprison the soul, or in excessive and exhaustive attention to minute detail. In helping the novices to gain interior liberty, Thérèse would make room in their souls for the Spirit. In demanding of them a daily humble fidelity, she teaches them to embody in the letter the spirit which alone vivifies.

3. Renunciation

Can the heart claim that it truly loves God if it still nourishes a thousand immortified appetites? Certainly not, and if to make room for the Lord, we must not constrict our souls, it is no less necessary to deny them many natural satisfactions, nourish them on a thousand sacrifices of love. Therefore, Thérèse asks for extreme vigilance in sacrifice in keeping with true interior freedom.

She has no intention of breaking the novices or of crushing their personalities. In exhorting them to renunciation, her only desire is to open their souls more fully to God, to permit supernatural desire to grow in them without measure. The young Mistress is strict in her requirements of sacrifice; intending to give her Sisters a solid formation, she would have them dead to all that is not God. She immediately rebukes them for all their failures, even punishes them severely while setting forth supernatural motives in stressing the positive side: love. Since a religious should have no other motives than supernatural ones, Thérèse presents only those to the novices to combat their natural inclinations. Such direction makes a lasting impression on souls.

"One feast day," a novice recounts, "in the refectory they forgot to give me, like the others, a dessert I especially liked. After dinner I went to see Sister Thérèse of the Child Jesus, and my neighbor at table was with her. I artfully made known her lack of attention.[21] Sister Thérèse heard me and made me go to the Sister

---

[20] E. p. 192.
[21] Each Carmelite is required, in the refectory, to see that the one beside her does not lack anything.

in charge of the refectory and ask for my dessert. I begged her not to impose this humiliation upon me.

" 'That will be your penance,' she answered severely; 'you are not worthy of the sacrifices that God asks of you. It was He Who permitted this forgetfulness and you betrayed His attention by complaining.'

" 'I can say,' the Sister concludes, 'that the lesson bore fruit for my whole life.' "[22]

Very often Thérèse had to remind her cousin, who sat beside her in the refectory, of the custody of the eyes. "You will never succeed in keeping your eyes lowered, if you do not mark each failure on your examen beads. That is the only way. . . . For the love of the good God, then, you do not wish to lower your eyes? Think that you are making an act of love each time that you do not raise them . . . that you are saving a soul."[23]

The saint's fidelity to the least religious customs needs no lengthy comment. It must be stressed that, for Thérèse, this vigilance is not the fruit of an entirely exterior application; it springs directly from the heart. What, indeed, would a purely formal observance be worth? Nothing! Contact with God is everything. The renunciation that Thérèse asks is simply an interior gaze wholly attentive to God. Love burns in her soul, and that is why this gaze is so penetrating and her fidelity in little things makes all, whether great or little, as one. It was not thus from the beginning.[24] From her own experience Thérèse knows that time and a solid formation are necessary to arrive at this attentiveness with ease. Also, without demanding an immediate perfection in this, she always emphasizes the spiritual motive for it.

Because "union with God is one of her particular recommendations,"[25] she reproves one novice who absent-mindedly hums a hymn, and another who, through inattention, sits sideways on her chair. Sadly, she says: "How many souls there are who do each action just about right or nearly so; how few who do everything as well as they possibly can!"[26]

---

[22] Circ. pp. 35–36.
[23] Quoted by Père Piat: "Marie Guerin," p. 73. [25] E. p. 99,
[24] S.S. p. 91; Ms. A, fol. 48 v°. [26] Ibid,

We have no right to forget God at any moment of the day. Thérèse asks the exhuberant Sister Marie of the Eucharist to deny herself in moments of relaxation: "Why do you go to recreation? To satisfy yourself and to find pleasure in it? One must go to it as faithfully as to any other community exercise, without ever stopping while going there. On leaving the refectory you should go at once to recreation; you do not have permission to stop for other things, not even for a single moment to speak to a Sister. . . . Then at recreation practice virtue, be pleasant with everyone, no matter who is near you. Be gay through virtue and not through caprice. When you are sad, forget yourself and show gaiety. Too often only pleasure is sought with no thought of practicing virtue, with no thought of occupying oneself with the good God. It is a community act like any other; enjoy it but especially in charity for others. Be watchful over yourself and remain virtuous even in the midst of pleasure. Make the sacrifice of not sitting next to those whom you like.

"Yes, you should always mortify yourself. It is good to be gay at recreation but there is a religious way of being gay, of entertaining others. Sometimes your gaiety is silliness and you think that that pleases the Sisters. They laugh at your foolishness, it is true, but it does not edify them. . . . Be charitable, attentive . . . oblige the seniors by finding chairs for them and at every opportunity be kind. A little novice should always do more than required. This would be so nice!"[27]

If Thérèse asks her novices to put their whole heart into what they do because "without love all is nothing,"[28] she strives still more, perhaps unnoticed, constantly to lift their hearts above created things. This is not the easiest form of self-denial. With good psychology she encourages the Sisters to live above the thousand trifles which take on so much importance under a Rule in a cloistered life. There the most insignificant unforeseen occurrences sometimes become like a tempest in a teapot, and the pursuit of trifles can submerge the desire for God, which alone should reign in souls. Thérèse works unceasingly to "exile"[29] her novices from their humble.

---

[27] Quoted by Père Piat: "Marie Guerin," p. 74.
[28] St. Teresa of Avila..   [29] Cf..M. p. 100..

tasks, to restore their perspective when she sees them engrossed in their work. That is not God; it should not distract them from Him!

"You are too much concerned with what you are doing;"[30] "you worry too much about your tasks. . . . Are you thinking at this moment of what is happening in other Carmels? Wondering if those religious are busy or not? Does their work interfere with your prayer and meditation? Well, then! In the same way you should be detached from your own work. Conscientiously give it the time required but with detachment of heart.[31] . . . We must work with one hand and with the other guard our souls against dissipation which prevents their union with God."[32]

But Thérèse goes still deeper. Not satisfied with helping her Sisters in their attitude or occupations, she wishes, particularly, to keep watch over their feelings and their too human way of thinking. She wishes the "old man" to be asleep before God so that true love may grow unhampered. The work is delicate, she knows, but essential. It is a matter of purifying the depths of the heart as much as possible, to prepare a clean place for the coming of God. Perhaps nowhere is Thérèse at the same time more gentle and more firm. Firm, she never allows self-seeking, however indirect or subtle it may be, without calling attention to the deviation. Gentle, she does not combat it head on nor is she scandalized; she explains, persuades, or simply expresses her thought, rekindling the desire to love.

When her cousin, too preoccupied with herself, confides some anxiety to her, Thérèse admonishes: "I beg you to be a little less occupied with yourself and concern yourself only with loving the good God. Your scruples are all self-seekings; your troubles and sorrows center upon yourself. Oh, I beg you, forget yourself and think of saving souls."[33]

She requires mortification of the affections,[34] of judgment,[35] of self-love, and that without restriction, certain that a soul who takes care of its natural life and follows all its inclinations is incapable

[30] E. p. 98.
[31] M. p. 100.
[32] M. p. 101.
[33] Quoted by Père Piat: "Marie Guerin," p. 86.
[34] S.S. p. 174.
[35] Cf. S.S. p. 297.

of seeking God, of living in Him as He wills. Such a soul has no understanding of the first step which led her to religion and of fidelity to her desire to love.

When still a novice, Thérèse said to a companion who was too naturally attached to the Mother Prioress, "If you must always behave so, you would have done better to remain in the world."[36] Nor does she speak differently when she is Mistress of Novices: "If you do not want to practice virtue, return to the world!" she asserts emphatically.[37]

She smiles at the naïve pretentions of her young Sisters; with a quiet word she restores true values and makes them realize the dependence of the creature and the infinity of God. One day a novice prided herself on having had her ideas accepted: "Oh!" exclaims Thérèse, "it pleases you to be well thought of. I prefer to repeat with our Lord: 'I seek not my own glory; someone else will take care of it.'"[38]

When her Sisters are anxious or grieved because of a judgment upon them, she is understanding but uncompromising: "When you are thought imperfect, that is necessary and it is your gain. . . . If others think you lacking in virtue, this does not deprive you of anything, nor are you any poorer. They lose in interior joy, for there is nothing sweeter than thinking well of our neighbor."[39] "The more you advance," she tells another, "the less you will have to struggle . . . your soul will rise above creatures. I am completely indifferent now as to what is said about me because I have understood the unreliability of human judgments. When we are misunderstood or harshly judged, what good is it to defend ourselves? We must pay no attention and say nothing, for it is so sweet to let oneself be judged, no matter how! The Gospel does not say that Saint Mary Magdalen defended herself when accused by her sister."[40] "We must rise above what the Sisters say, what they do . . . we must live in our monastery as though we were to spend only two days there."[41]

---

[36] Quoted by Père Petitot in "Une Renaissance Spirituelle," p. 218.
[37] Sum. Ext. from the deposition of Sr. Mary-Magdalen of the Blessed Sacrament, kindly communicated by the Carmel of Lisieux.
[38] E. p. 91.
[39] M. pp. 27–28.
[40] S.S. pp. 311–312.
[41] Sum.

Human occupations, human quests, everything that is not God is unimportant. God alone matters! Thérèse guides her novices toward Him alone, through all that is external and amidst snares. She is not less attentive in directing their spiritual activity. She desires souls to be attached only to God; self-denial will purify all intentions. To those who think of a retreat as a time to rest, Thérèse says: "You are going into retreat to rest? I go in the hope of giving more to the good God. . . . Remember what the *Imitation* so rightly says: 'As soon as a soul begins to seek itself, it ceases to love.' "[42]

Another asks her about spiritual direction: "I think," Thérèse says, "it is good to be on guard, to avoid self-seeking, lest the heart be wounded and then we shall say with truth: 'The keepers . . . wounded me . . . [and] took away my veil from me. When I had a little passed by them, I found him whom my soul loveth. . . .'[43] If the soul humbly asks the keepers where her Beloved is, they will tell her, but if she wants to impress others, she will fall into trouble; she will lose simplicity of heart."[44]

Thérèse does not scruple in denying her Sisters their seemingly holiest pursuits. A novice who wished to remember passages from Scripture to nourish her piety was told: "You want riches and possessions! Leaning on these things is like leaning on a red-hot iron; it will leave a little scar! We must lean on *nothing*, not even on the things we think may help our piety. Let us seek only truth; let us have no wish nor hope of sensible joy. Then shall we be truly happy! 'Where is the man' asks the *Imitation*, 'that is wholly divested of all self-seeking?' "[45]

She brought the same purity of intention to her reception of the sacraments. "I offered myself to Jesus, not as a person who longs to receive His visit for her own consolation, but for the pleasure of Him Who gives Himself to me."[46]

She advised her Sisters to do likewise, not to communicate for their own satisfaction, but because Jesus loves to give Himself. "Jesus is in the tabernacle expressly for you, for you alone. He longs

[42] E. p. 38.
[43] Cant. 5:7; 3:4.
[44] N.V. pp. 63–64.

[45] Doc.; M. pp. 32–33; see p. 39, fn. 5.
[46] S.S. p. 142; Ms. A, fol. 79 v°.

to come into your heart."⁴⁷ "Do not be troubled at feeling no consolation in your communions; that is a trial to be borne with love."⁴⁸

Carrying renunciation even into their relations with God, Thérèse prepares souls for an authentic spiritual life. Her great care is to erase what is human, depending on the novices' ardent longing for Jesus. She speaks of renunciation only in view of union with God; thus conceived, it seems indispensable to her for it allows the divine work, which alone matters. "Our God," she states, "our heart's Guest, knows it well (that we can do nothing of ourselves), so He comes to us intending to find a dwelling place, an empty tent, in the midst of the world's battlefield. He asks only that," and will Himself undertake the rest.⁴⁹

Such teaching commits one to the absolute. Thérèse demands of her novices an interior ascesis that is more exacting, more formidable to nature than all penances. She teaches them to turn aside from the nothingness of all creation, to make "place for the Uncreated which is reality";⁵⁰ she accustoms them to live only under the gaze of God. She goes to the very roots, which will produce external, visible, precious fruits. Souls formed from the outset according to such principles need only to live them to be above all human fluctuations.⁵¹

They will test these principles, but they will not stop there because God will be their All. With a gaze fixed on Him who does not change, they will not feel incapacitated the day they leave the Novitiate; they will be more fully surrendered to Him. Their new life and its responsibilities will not find them shaken by every wind of doctrine, or turning back upon themselves, but virile, conscious of the true value of things, and capable of acting in everything entirely through love. Of what importance are the tasks given them to do, of what importance is a change of Superior or monastery? (And often these are painful and confusing sacrifices, even for a soul solidly established in Religion.) Desiring to renounce themselves without reserve and certain that the best means are

---

⁴⁷ L. p. 107.
⁴⁸ L. p. 110.
⁴⁹ L. p. 231.

⁵⁰ L. p. 143.
⁵¹ See Appendix (Penance and Health).

nothing in themselves, they will pass by all, simple and strong, seeking only their God.

This is a fruitful formation which gives souls an initial impulse, which is so powerful and so pure, that it is sufficient for them to follow it all their life to be faithful to God and to fulfill their measure of grace. It is a valuable formation which prepares them for all love's invasions and future demands; yet this is still no more than an entrance into the spiritual life.

CHAPTER V

Faith in Love, Foundation of the Way of Childhood

THÉRÈSE strives untiringly to bring the novices to the All of God and the nothingness of creatures, to arouse in them a sincere desire to love Jesus and to live for Him alone. The Mistress is convinced that without this firm and pure will nothing can be done, but that once this generous orientation is established, the work is well begun and the highest hopes for the advancement of souls are justified.

The time comes when it is necessary to give to this desire a solid support and food at every moment. When a soul has made the first necessary efforts of renunciation, God tests it. Thérèse sees her novices exposed to many difficulties, through which she must guide them to the stable and permanent union of love. Now faith in Love dominates.

1. The Love in Which Thérèse Believes

Thérèse makes an ardent effort to discern the face of Love leaning toward her. She desires to know Him, always to love Him more and make Him loved as He deserves. Although she has not written a treatise on love, it illumines every page of her writings in vibrant lines in the *Letters* and in *The Story of a Soul*.

PERSONAL LOVE

First and foremost, it is a person-to-person love. God is in Himself more real and more personal than anything imaginable in our universe. We merit to be called persons only because of the grace of our resemblance to the Creator. This God, this transcendent Personality, is also Love, who makes Himself more intimate to us than we are to ourselves! The fruit of the first mystical graces reveals God to our souls as One who loves us. But in our daily, material life, it is so easy to let this precious knowledge be lost.

Thérèse fervently clings to God and lives intimately with Him in a ceaseless heart-to-heart: "I believe I have never been three minutes without thinking of the good God."[1] She knows that God, the Creator and Father, dwells in the depths of her being and that He, the All-Powerful, the infinitely Wise and Good, places all His power, wisdom and goodness at the service of His love for her. Thérèse sees clearly that the secondary causes He uses are inseparable from the unique and All-loving First Cause: "When something happens [she is speaking of herself] one must see only the gentle hand of Jesus."[2]

For Thérèse God is Jesus and Jesus is her All. She lives with Him in the closest intimacy. In her secret prayer[3] to Him she prefers to use the familiar "tu."[4] She unites herself to the mysteries of His childhood and, above all, of His suffering. Living the life which He imparts to her, the saint penetrates the divine Persons. In her last years one discerns a very marked movement of soul toward the Holy Trinity.[5] She seems to live in a special and different relation with each of the Three Persons. Her living faith wins for her the highest earthly union: "I do not see that I shall have more after my death than I possess now. . . . I shall see the good God, that is true! But as to being with Him, I am already with Him upon earth."[6]

But if Thérèse loves God as a Friend, living and close at hand, she is also conscious of being loved by Him in a very special manner. The divine Heart beats for her personally: "I do not see the Sacred Heart as others do. I believe that the Heart of my Spouse

---

[1] Sum. p. 1626; M. p. 104.
[2] Cf. L. p. 145.
[3] Cf. M. p. 110.
[4] "Tu" is the second person pronoun used in addressing dear ones, rather than "vous," which is formal.
[5] She addressed her Act of Offering to the Triune God on the Feast of the Holy Trinity; see also S.S. p. 148; fol. 5 v°; S.S. p. 447; M. p. 93; Ms. B.
[6] N.V. pp. 1–2.

is for me alone, as mine is for Him alone, and then I speak with Him in the solitude of this delightful intimacy while waiting to behold Him face to face."[7]

The relations of Jesus and Thérèse are reciprocal, vibrant, mutually tender, with no other care than to gratify the Beloved, to prefer the Beloved to all. "O my Jesus, it may be an illusion but it seems to me that You could never fill a soul with more love than You have filled mine. . . . I cannot conceive a greater love than You have lavished on me gratuitously *without any merit on my part.*"[8]

INFINITE LOVE

All souls may say this: God, being infinite, can love only infinitely. His gifts differ but not the love with which He gives them, which is always "the tenderness of His infinite love."[9] Which is more important, the giving or the gift? Whether one be rich or poor, exalted or humbled in men's eyes, the saint is convinced that God holds each one infinitely dear. "Even as the sun shines at the same time on the cedar and on every little flower as though it were the only one on earth, so too, our Lord is concerned with each soul . . . and everything contributes to its good."[10]

Thérèse, therefore, can truly say to each of her Sisters: "Jesus loves you with all His heart."[11] "Oh, yes, Jesus loves you."[12] And with even more conviction: "The good God loves you and treats you as a privileged one. . . ."[13]

GRATUITOUS LOVE

Moreover, divine love is not only infinite but it is wholly gratuitous, "without any merit on our part."[14] Thérèse realizes that "there is nothing in her worthy of attracting His divine glances."[15] How can God love us? she asks. What do we offer Him to cherish? "Question full of mysteries. . . . What reason can Jesus give us? . . . His reason is that He has no reason." . . .[16] Nothing but His free choice could make Him love the creature, for God does not love

---

[7] L. pp. 152–153.
[8] S.S. p. 192; Ms. C, fol. 35 r°.
[9] S.S. p. 198; Ms. B, fol. 1 v°.
[10] S.S. p. 31; Ms. A, fol. 3 r°.
[11] L. p. 314.

[12] L. p. 314.
[13] L. p. 129.
[14] Cf. S.S. p. 192; Ms. C, fol. 35 r°.
[15] S.S. p. 32; Ms. A, fol. 3 v°.
[16] L. p. 100.

in a human manner. Man loves what he finds lovable in another. God loves what He has given us. We have only this to draw His love.

If such is the love of God, independent of our mediocrity and our faults, what confident peace we should have! What we are is a mystery, but a mystery of love. Is it not ridiculous to judge divine love according to our human love? How much better to listen to Thérèse!

There is still one last characteristic of love which has captivated the saint even more strongly and which has definitely illumined her life. This Love in which she believes and to which she guides souls is, above all, Merciful Love.[17]

LOVE WHICH CLAIMS LOVE IN RETURN

". . . Let us therefore love, because God first loved us."[18] Thérèse shares St. John's conclusion. In studying the heart of God, Thérèse has discovered the fundamental requirement of love. She has received the inestimable grace of understanding "how much Jesus desires to be loved."[19] Because she has believed in divine charity, the saint has believed still more, if we can say it, in God's insatiable thirst for a return of His love, for the love of each soul to whom He gives Himself. "Jesus is thirsty for love."[20] "He wants our love, He begs for it . . . He seems to place Himself at our mercy. He wants nothing that we do not willingly give Him and the smallest thing is precious in His sight" . . . [21] Thérèse is certain that to be loved is to be infinitely desired, and she knows that Jesus seeks her love, that He demands her whole heart.

This ardent invitation of love, boundless and unreasoning, has been the light of Thérèse's life and her most effective means of formation. One can say that the saint believed in love and love alone; in love as the source of all life, as the means of perfection and a staff for the journey; in love as the sole end. On her deathbed

---

[17] As the discovery of mercy in its infinite depth determines for the Mistress the full flowering of the spiritual life, we shall study this aspect of love more particularly in the following chapter.

[18] 1 Jn. 4:19.

[19] S.S. p. 148; Ms. A, fol. 84 r°.

[20] S.S. p. 198; Ms. B, fol. 1 v°.

[21] L. p. 197.

she affirms: "I have said all . . . it is love alone that counts."[22]
This is all one needs to understand; this supernatural conviction is
communicated to souls who draw near to it.

2. Faith in Love

Having helped her novices to know divine Love, Thérèse now
wants them to have faith in Love. In her opinion, what is the role
and nature of this faith?

Thérèse assigns it a fundamental role in the spiritual life. Without faith in Love, the soul's desire for God would wither like a plant
in shallow earth.

Life on earth is an exercise of faith. But faith in Love as seen
by Thérèse, the faith which the spiritual life calls for, is immeasur-
ably rich and fruitful. Intellectual belief in revealed truths is not
enough; we must believe with our whole being in God's love, in
His ways and in His promises. Closely analyzed, the attitude that
Thérèse demands is obviously not the particular act of one isolated
theological virtue, faith, hope or charity, but rather, the act of a
loving faith clinging closely to God and awaiting all from Him
because He is love. This faith in Love, characterizing spiritual childhood and evangelical virtue, is a very simple movement of the soul
but, like everything that Thérèse demands, it is an essential.

Upon a naked, living, total faith, Thérèse intends to lay the
foundations of the spiritual life. The soul's true and permanent
support in its desire for God may be only a faith that rests in God
alone in His immutable love, a faith become immutable like Him.

Thérèse is not unaware that God has filled the souls of her
Sisters with His sweetness, that they have enjoyed the sense of
His loving presence. But she also knows that God seems to withdraw
when He wishes to strengthen them, and that, almost as soon as
they cross the threshold of the cloister. And the Mistress, who
knows from experience the divine tactics, relies upon past graces,
upon the impression they have left in the soul, when their savor
disappears.

"And we have come to know, and have believed, the love that
God has in our behalf," says St. John.[23] The souls who have

[22] N.V. p. 135. [23] 1 Jn. 4:16.

received from Christ the most intimate call to follow Him have experienced His love, and the desire to respond to it has brought them into Religion. But when this desire is put to the test, it seems close to breaking. The thought that God is All no longer inflames them; it may even oppress them. The certitude of the call received disappears. The consciousness of their wretchedness increases in the confused souls; the moments of fatigue, of wear and tear, of temptation, pile up. The pursuit of perfection seems an illusion; prayer seems an utter loss, both of strength and of time. The suffering souls become contracted and strained.

Thérèse tries to sustain them without breaking them; to raise their minds and wills above the transitory, the sweet or the bitter, and center them on eternal divine charity. The novices' faith formerly rested on God's love as they had personally known it; now it rests on remembrance of that love. Thérèse's unshakable certainty will sustain the spiritual edifice that God has begun to raise in their souls. Past graces help the novices to preserve their confidence in spite of present aridity. Thérèse would have them use their trial to attain a faith which no longer needs consolation, a faith similar to hers, needing only truth. "It is in the spirit of my little way to desire to see nothing . . ."[24] "I prefer to live by faith."[25] And even more firmly: "I have desired more not to see God and the saints and to remain in the night of faith, than others have desired to see all and to understand all."[26] Thérèse wants to convince her companions, that having received so many graces from God, they should be too certain of His love to ask for sensible proofs of it, or to take pleasure in consolations rather than in the substance of the supernatural life. "It is so sweet to serve the good God in darkness and trial. We have only this life to live by faith."[27] In the school of Thérèse it is essential to believe in God Himself, to desire God for Himself without stopping at anything less than God. In the mind of the saint only such a desire and such a faith attain to the measure of God, who is infinite love.

Sufficient work has been done, from the negative standpoint, in establishing souls above their sensible impressions. From this naked

24 N.V. p. 14.
25 N.V. p. 126.
26 N.V. p. 96.
27 M. p. 197.

faith she wishes to make a living faith; as she strives to despoil it, she works also to nourish it. Since her Sisters sincerely desire to love God, they must convince themselves that everything that happens to them comes from Love; any event, however disappointing or repugnant it may seem, can never be an obstacle to love. Everything is a means of going to Him. "Now we know that for those who love God all things work together unto good, for those who, according to his purpose, are saints through his call."[28] Once established in this faith, one's whole spiritual life is assured; without this faith there is only despair, delusion, or mediocrity.

This explains the extreme importance of the direction given at this point by spiritual guides. It is difficult to remove the attachment of a soul accustomed to judging according to the senses and to teach it to love with facility, when it suddenly finds itself faced with the naked truth, severed from sensible love and obliged to work in aridity and darkness! It is nevertheless here that St. Thérèse's talent for direction is shown to be most reliable.

Where do all these trials come from? Why this obscurity after light? In the springtime of their spiritual life the novices knew the love with which they were loved; now they need to know themselves as they are. That is the source of their sufferings. The Love which enlightened them on Himself enlightens them today on their poverty. Without this previous knowledge they could not have borne the sight of their miseries. It is only to reveal Himself better that, with seeming cruelty, He reveals the impure depths of their souls. Let them not lose sight of Love, for to do so is to compromise the whole work; let them never cease to look steadfastly at Him and soon the light will completely and forever reveal Love as Mercy. This is, for Thérèse, the supreme teaching.

3. The Counsels of Thérèse

Far from being lost in theory, her counsels are precise and practical.

Preserved in the *Letters* and *Recollections*, Thérèse's method corresponds with what she knows of Love; to fix one's gaze upon God and transform both joys and sorrows into love. These are the

---

[28] Rom. 8:28.

complementary aspects of the soul's one action, faith in love. In the first, intellect and will are lost in God and seem particularly adapted to sustain the life of prayer; the second aims at making the best use of all that is created for the service of God. Thérèse uses both to strengthen the novices in their certainty of being loved and in the certainty that God desires and accepts their love. (She also uses the desire to win souls. But, as we know, for her, this apostolic love is one with the love of God.)

Such a simplification is indispensable during this period of the spiritual life, even if it was not previously. This is no longer the time to deal severely with the novice's faults. God is doing that sufficiently! Now it is necessary to remove the multiplicity which would uselessly fatigue them. Thérèse does not deny the miseries that her Sisters discover in themselves; but she puts them under the light of faith declaring that their unsightliness is all the more reason to look at Love. Neither does she deny their suffering, nor pretend that it is light, but she teaches them to love Him who sends it to them through love. Finally, neither does she deny that our neighbor's conduct can cause pain or sadness. But she teaches that we must love him as he is, see our Lord in him and show him the same love as Christ does. In faith the soul soars to love.

THE GAZE OF FAITH UPON LOVE

In an unforgettable letter to her sister, Marie, Thérèse symbolizes the whole life of faith as she understands it: it is "the story of her little bird."[29] She describes the fervent disposition of the soul held firmly by faith in love and moved by an immense desire to love. "In spite of my extreme littleness, I dare to gaze upon the divine sun, the sun of Love, and my heart feels within it all the eagle's aspirations."[30]

Then she reviews in her own way the different obstacles which souls encounter in their flight toward God; she triumphs over everything by demanding this gaze on Love. Whether it is physical weakness which makes her fall asleep during prayer,[31] or moral helplessness and miseries which prevent her from rising to God,[32] or

---

29 Cf. L. p. 283.   31 L. p. 285.
30 L. p. 284.   32 Cf. L. p. 285.

infidelities which remove her from Him;[33] or, finally, whether it is spiritual disorders, trials, temptations, and obscurities,[34] she teaches that there is only one thing to do: believe that this does not prevent Love from remaining what He is and continue to gaze at Him; return to Him as soon as one is conscious of having strayed from Him; lastly, hope for all from this irresistible Love from whom we receive all good things.

"With daring abandonment it (the little bird) wishes to remain gazing upon its divine sun. Nothing frightens it, neither wind nor rain and, if dark clouds come to hide the star of love, the little bird does not change its place; it knows that beyond the clouds its sun always shines and its brilliance will not know an instant's eclipse."[35]

Thus Thérèse wants faith to be fed and strengthened by every obstacle, to cling so strongly to the transcendence of divine love that it may establish the soul above all interior and exterior vicissitudes.

To Transform All Into Love

Thérèse knows how difficult it is to make a soul go out of herself, when everything conspires to turn her thoughts back upon herself. Thérèse puts love in the center of all preoccupations and fosters forgetfulness of self. Believe in love, she says, and transform into love all that constrains, afflicts, or tortures you. Since it has its source in the infinite love of Jesus for you, you should believe that in this trial, this doubt, this temptation, He awaits your love. All this He permits only that He may receive a new proof, a greater, purer proof, of your love.

Thérèse wishes to convince her Sisters that God puts an infinite value on their response during the difficult times when they are incapable of love, or doubt that their poor and weak love could be pleasing to Him. The night of trial, wherein they experience their helplessness, is the best time for love; they must profit by it like "misers."[36]

When her novices or her Sisters come to her deploring their

---

[33] L. p. 285.   [35] L. p. 284.
[34] Cf. L. p. 284. [36] L. p. 120.

defects or weaknesses, Thérèse's only reply is an encouragement to strengthen themselves in love.

A novice says: "I am grieved by my lack of courage!" "You complain," replies her Mistress, "of what should be your greatest happiness. Where would be your merit if you had to struggle only when you felt courage? What does it matter that you do not have any, provided that you act as though you did? If you are too faint-hearted to pick up a piece of thread but do it for the love of Jesus, you have more merit than if you had performed a much greater action in a moment of fervor. Instead of being sad, rejoice. By letting you feel your weakness, Jesus gives you an opportunity to save a greater number of souls for Him."[37] Thérèse does not stop there; from the faults themselves and from the sadness they feel, she would have them draw love.

To Mother Agnes, who confided some discouraging thoughts, the saint says: "I try never to be discouraged. When I have committed a fault which makes me sad, I know that this sadness is the consequence of my unfaithfulness. But do you think I stop there? Oh, no! I hasten to say to the good God: 'My God, I know that I have deserved this feeling of sadness; let me offer it to You anyway, as a trial which You have sent me through love. I am sorry for what I have done but I am glad to have this suffering to offer to You.' "[38]

Interior trials and temptations are "occasions to prove her love for Jesus."[39] She knows souls; in hours of doubt and weariness, it is as difficult to believe in the reality of our love for God, as to believe in His love for us. "God loves me, I know," a tearful novice may say, "but I don't love Him!" Love is supernatural and the supernatural is above the domain of the senses. Love proceeds from our will informed by grace; each time that we will to love, we really love.[40] No less faith is needed to believe that our unfelt love is pleasing to God, than to believe in His love for us.

Thérèse's purpose is to establish souls in this certitude, beyond

---

[37] S.S. p. 309.
[38] N.V. p. 26.
[39] S.S. p. 308.
[40] This supposes the practice of the movement of abandonment explained in Chapter VIII.

all impressions. She strengthens and nurtures the desire to love at the moment when it is directly attacked in the soul. Teaching her companions never to judge their degree of union with God according to their feelings of fervor or aridity, she bids them to cling in mind and will to the love He offers them. She strives to make them understand that union with God is no more than a perfect conformity of views, desires and will; the soul forgets herself completely for Him whom she loves. In mystical union she can, if it pleases God, enjoy the presence of her Beloved and the joy of His intimacy. In practical and hidden union she is truly His without any recompense; in the purity of a love stronger than death she lives entirely from His grace. This union, however, is not so hidden from the soul that it does not give, at least at times, a minimum of mystical graces, indicating that our Lord takes pleasure in this hidden love; there is a certainty of mind, a tenderness of will, a deep movement of soul, a feeling that it is wholly possessed by God. "Jesus hides Himself but the soul divines His Presence."[41]

When a generous soul understands that on earth she must be concerned with love in faith, when she desires this solid union, she has progressed far. No longer for herself but for His sake the soul desires Jesus. Thérèse, co-operating with grace, has removed all accessories from the souls in her charge and permits them only the purest, truest desire to love. The useless falls away in the force of the impulse toward love.

The supernatural desire is now so ardent that nothing can satisfy it. In the name of all her Sisters Thérèse may write: "Understanding that the thirst which consumes you is a thirst of love, we would wish to possess an infinite love to quench it."[42]

By surrendering souls to Love, the saint initiates the last step which opens to them an intense and stable spiritual life.

---

[41] L. p. 56.
[42] S.S. p. 450, Prayer composed for the Novitiate.

CHAPTER VI

The Offering to Love, the Definitive Engagement

WHILE the soul in trial sees her wretchedness and preserves a sincere desire to love God and a living faith in love, the Mistress comes to help her persevere by proposing that she surrender herself to Merciful Love. Through this act one's being is possessed to its depths, and true spiritual life begins. Hence, St. Thérèse hastens to guide each soul to this surrender as soon as possible.

Without the sincere supernatural desire to love God, the invitation to self-surrender would be meaningless and would lead only to laziness; without absolute faith in love, the invitation would be in vain. But these qualities may be present in a soul at the beginning of the spiritual life: in a newly converted sinner or in an imperfect soul, filled with faults and even evil tendencies or subject to serious lapses.

1. *Merciful Love*

By offering herself unreservedly to Merciful Love, so unappreciated by men, Thérèse hopes to draw after her a "great number of little souls."[1] It is not necessary to have arrived at an advanced state of holiness to surrender oneself; still better, this donation has an educational value. Since only Jesus may direct souls, Thérèse wants the souls of her novices open to Him at the earliest possible moment.

Hardly has she conceived her plan to offer herself and obtained permission from Reverend Mother Agnes, than she shares it with Celine and asks her to join her in making it; she does not keep

---
[1] Cf. S.S. p. 208; Ms. B, fol. 5 v°.

her secret for herself alone. On June 11, 1895, she pronounces the Act of Offering for herself and Sister Genevieve (Celine), who had entered Carmel only ten months previously. Shortly afterward, she invites her eldest sister, Sister Marie of the Sacred Heart, to do likewise.[2]

With Sister Marie of the Trinity she acted with more prudence. (Through the *Conseils et Souvenirs* and the Circular Letter of the Lisieux Carmel, this young Sister is well known to us.) It is almost six months later that Thérèse tells her about this oblation. With generosity the novice "immediately manifested the desire to imitate her and it was decided that she would make her consecration the following day."[3]

Lively and spontaneous, rather childish, enthusiastic yet quickly dejected, sensitive and quick to tears, eager to be loved and esteemed, grieving over her wretchedness and extremely fearful of God's judgment, but deeply trusting her Mistress, Sister Marie of the Trinity was not a ready-made Carmelite. What good was there in her at this time? A sincere desire to love Jesus and a deep conviction of her many weaknesses. Thérèse had guessed right that she need but reveal to her novice her own donation to love to lead her to take the same step.

But when she was alone and reflected upon her unworthiness, the novice concluded that a longer time of preparation was necessary for an act of such importance. She returned to Sister Thérèse of the Child Jesus to explain the reasons why she should defer her offering.

"Yes," the saint agreed, "this act is more important than we can imagine. But do you know the only preparation that the good God asks of us? It is a humble recognition of our unworthiness. Oh! Since He has given you this grace, abandon yourself to Him without fear. Tomorrow morning, after thanksgiving, I shall remain near you in the oratory where the Blessed Sacrament will be exposed; while you pronounce this act, I will offer you to Jesus as the little victim which I prepared for Him."[4]

While possessing a stronger and purer thirst for love, the novices

---

[2] M. p. 90.   [4] Circ. pp. 31–32.
[3] Circ. p. 31.

whom Thérèse surrenders to Him also possess a deeper knowledge of their own miseries. And this knowledge, which might sometimes deter them on their flight toward God, is the very condition, Thérèse declares, for the offering to Merciful Love. Her letter to Sister Marie of the Sacred Heart expresses exactly the same idea:

"Understand that to love Jesus, to be His victim of love, the weaker one is, without desires or virtues[5] [it is a question here of desires for martyrdom or the accomplishment of great things], the better one is fitted for the work of this consuming and transforming love.

What, then, is Merciful Love, that such a preparation should be fitting for Him? Thérèse has a keen understanding of divine mercy; it is the mark of her soul. "He has given me His infinite mercy and through it I contemplate and adore the other divine perfections! . . . Then everything seems radiant with love."[6]

God loves us with mercy, that is to say, He loves us despite our miseries and numberless faults. He measures His demands according to His knowledge of our strength: "He takes account of our weaknesses, He knows perfectly the frailty of our nature."[7]

---

[5] The meaning of the expression "without desires or virtues" is clarified by the context. As M. Abbé Combes has judiciously remarked in his edition of the Collected Letters of Saint Thérèse of Lisieux: The expression "without desires" cannot be taken literally because it is said further: "The sole desire to be a victim suffices," which presupposes that one is not "without virtues," but already animated by a very great theological charity.

For Thérèse, as she explains at the beginning of the same letter, "to be without desires" is to keep oneself from the spiritual vanity which could easily creep into our plans of sanctity: "My desires for martyrdom are nothing. . . . They are, to tell the truth, the spiritual riches which could make us unjust if we rest in them complacently and think they are something great. . . . Oh! I realize that it is not that which pleases the good God in my soul. What pleases Him is to see me love my littleness and poverty, the blind hope I have in His mercy. . . . There is my sole treasure."

Thérèse speaks of virtues in these terms on August 6, 1897: ". . . To be little, moreover, is not to attribute to ourselves the virtues we practice, nor to believe ourselves capable of anything, but to recognize that the good God puts this treasure of virtue into the hands of His little child to be used in time of need but it is always the treasure of the good God." N.V. p. 80.

Above all one must have confidence: "In a sense the saint was 'without desires or virtues.' She did not rely for support upon those which God had gratuitously granted her. She was truly poor." P. Lucien-Marie de St. Joseph quoted by M. Abbé Combes in his edition of the Collected Letters of Saint Thérèse of Lisieux, p. 289.

[6] S.S. p. 147; Ms. A, fol. 83 v°.   [7] S.S. p. 147; Ms. A, fol. 83 v°.

Thérèse goes still deeper: God not only loves us despite our miseries and takes them into account, but He loves us because of them, knowing, like a very loving father, that the greater our weakness the more we need His love. "God," she says, "always finds our miserable straws and our most insignificant actions beautiful."[8]

For Thérèse, mercy manifests itself not only in the pardons which God multiplies for us, but also in the paternal solicitude with which He disposes all things for us. Consequently, the saint, who has not committed a mortal sin, considers herself, even more than a converted sinner, the object of divine mercy which prevented her from falling by removing all obstacles from her path.[9] Love is, therefore, the same for all souls; to those who trust in Him, He "forgives all,"[10] either in advance or after a fall. Thérèse has understood that God is always merciful in His relations with us. It is the normal consequence of what He is and of what we are. Love, insofar as it inclines God toward sinners, is and can be only mercy. In truth, God's mercy is His love at work in our regard. The entire Redemption is only the movement of merciful love, or, if one prefers, of gratuitous love, which comes to save sinners[11] by incorporating them in Jesus Christ, by making them live the divine life.

One sees to what a remarkable degree Thérèse has grasped the spirit of the Redemption, in the sense that St. Paul speaks of it in the Epistle to the Romans. She does not seek, like St. Augustine, to humble man in order to exalt the work of God. It is needless to prove our misery; this is glaringly evident. Thérèse has experienced it and thus teaches others. But if St. Paul insists that the aim of the law which clearly reveals our sin to us is to induce man to cast himself into the arms of God, if the Apostle describes the ravages of sin throughout history, as well as in the most intimate depths of our divided hearts, it is to magnify the Redemption, for the more sin increases, the more grace superabounds. ". . . God commends his charity toward us, because when as yet we were sinners, Christ died for us."[12] Thérèse echoes this magnificent and consoling doctrine and draws from it to direct souls.

---

[8] M. p. 76.
[9] Cf. S.S. p. 79; Ms. C, fol. 36 v°; N.V. p. 40.
[10] Cf. S.S. p. 79; Ms. A, fol. 39 r°.
[11] Cf. Lk. 1:78.
[12] Rom. 5:8–9.

Why wait until the novices no longer have any faults to surrender them to Merciful Love? Thérèse surrenders them to Him *because they are* full of miseries which they themselves are incapable of correcting. She warns them that Love will work in them only on one condition: that they consent "to remain always poor and without strength";[13] they must love their helplessness and unceasingly offer it to the Savior. Thérèse names only one condition for the efficacy of the offering, the same condition that God gave for the fruitfulness of the Redemption: true humility in the knowledge of self, in faith, confidence and love.

2. The Offering to Love

But what is surrender to Love? Thérèse is asked: "Is it sufficient to make the act of offering you composed?" "Oh, no," she replies, "words are not sufficient. To be truly a victim of love, you must surrender yourself totally. We are consumed by love only in the measure of our self-surrender."[14] No, a single act cannot do all, nor can words, no matter how sublime they are! Thérèse's doctrine is no less exacting than the New Testament on which it is based. Fundamentally, her spirituality has a living faith in the reality of grace and the experimental knowledge of our fallen nature. If God has grafted in us His own life, if He has endowed us with a complete and delicate spirituality of grace, the virtues and the gifts, Thérèse thinks that such talents should not remain unproductive. Although the Holy Spirit personally makes Himself the Guest of our soul, she does not believe that He intends to dwell there inactive. She feels that He infinitely desires to take possession of His creature, to see it surrendered to His complete direction.

But whereas the divine life is there, ready to flow into nature, nature too often resists the infusion of grace because of the frustration of our sensibility. Indeed, our fall is not an inspiring reality. Inclined by the burden of the body toward earthly and sensible things, man retains a jealous inclination to bring everything back to himself, a fierce claim to autonomy, a disordered restlessness.

Two lives, entirely different and often opposed, coexist in us, yet one is made to inform the other. Thérèse, thirsting for the absolute,

---

[13] L. p. 289.   [14] S.S. p. 311.

instinctively places herself and her novices before this dualism which, if compromised, would thwart the divine life. She has seen nature's innate tendency to live for and by itself. Although so innocent and so young, she is not mistaken about our human condition and about the inner anguish St. Paul so perceptively analyzed: ". . . I do not the good that I wish, but the evil that I do not wish, that I perform."[15] But Thérèse also understood the infinite mercy of God which, given the liberty, takes over the entire activity of His creature; as she desires to be a saint and to love unto folly, she has only to put herself into the hands of God. "I want to be a saint but I feel my powerlessness and I ask You, O my God, to be Yourself my Sanctity . . . I feel in my heart boundless desires and with confidence I ask You to come and take possession of my soul."[16]

Total surrender to Love requires a constant disposition of heart, keeping it free, receptive, and thirsty for the overflowing plenitude of God who gives Himself to us and who redeems us. This deep and continuous movement of soul means absolute dependence on Love. Since Mercy is Love in action, to surrender to Love is to place ourselves in His hands, to give free rein to the divine initiative. Lastly, it is to establish God in place of our "self" at the root of all our activity.

Thérèse has reached the heart of the problem. The question is not if movement, if life, will remain in our natural faculties. We know by experience that these do not fail and that their suppression does not constitute Christian holiness. But the question is, where will this vital movement begin? Immediately Thérèse replies: from God alone, always from God. Knowing that God can direct this and desires to do so, she invites Him, surrenders herself to Him and leaves it in His hands. "With what sweetness I have returned my will to Him! Yes, I want Him to take charge of my faculties in such a way that my actions will no longer be human and personal but divine, inspired and directed by the Spirit of Love."[17]

Elsewhere, commenting on St. Paul, " 'We do not know what we should pray for as we ought, but the Spirit himself pleads for

---

[15] Rom. 7:19.   [17] S.S. p. 318.
[16] Act of Offering, L. pp. 373–374.

us with unutterable groanings': we, therefore have only to surrender our soul, to abandon it to our great God."[18]

A soul thus surrendered, as soon as it is conscious of the too natural activity of her faculties, will gently restrain them when they instinctively assume too much independence. To mortify the impulse of nature by a simple gaze at God or the Virgin (Thérèse does both impartially), by a contact resumed in prayer, be it only for a second, or by purifying the intention, is to yield to grace, to give it the command it should have over all human activity.

This is also to practice complete interior renunciation, which puts the ego to death more rapidly than any other practice, since it attacks the ego, not in its manifestations, but in its depths; it puts the ax to the root of the tree. If, in the beginning, renunciation took other forms and seemed more precise, it was, in reality, less exacting. Made up of a succession of acts it became almost a state. Henceforth renunciation consists in an interior movement toward love, not straining for or against a given act; it feeds, without interruption and without distraction, the stream of love and life which flows from God into the soul.

3. The New Life

Thérèse has promised that surrender to Love satisfies one's great desire to love God, even amidst miseries. In fact, the offering to Love begins with this fundamental, precise intention: "In order to live in an act of perfect love. . . ."[19] So Thérèse not only claims by this surrender to love better but to live in an act of perfect love. Is this not a foolish, impossible ambition? She does not think so. "'My Father works even until now, and I work,' "[20] said our Lord to the Pharisees who were scandalized to see Him perform miracles on the Sabbath day. God likewise works without ceasing in a peaceful soul which is totally detached from herself and surrendered to Him. He even acts when the soul's attention is not continually fixed on Him — which is impossible to our human weakness — provided only that it is faithful in offering itself and, in all its natural activity, remaining in that state of peaceful dependence in

---

[18] Rom. 8:26; L. p. 231.   [20] Jn. 5:17.
[19] S.S. p. 448, Act of Offering; Ms. Appendix.

which God is pleased to work. Nothing is easier to Love, who dwells in the soul, than to continually act on it, even without its knowledge, if it is abandoned to Him. No longer with its own love does the soul love God but with the divine Heart itself. This is the love to which Thérèse aspires, the love that she wishes for her Sisters and for all little souls.

"Love attracts love, my Jesus, and mine, as it darts toward You, would wish to fill the Abyss which draws it, but alas! it is not even a dewdrop lost in the ocean. To love You as You love me, I must borrow Your own love; then only do I find peace."[21]

For a surrendered soul, faith in Love becomes faith in the unceasing action of Love in her. Possessing her heart, God secretly accomplishes His consuming and transforming work in it. We cannot repeat too often that Thérèse did not ordinarily feel God's action, but she truly believed in it. This intimate possession, hidden even from the one possessed, seems to her as "the truest and the holiest sanctity."[22]

Nevertheless, the surrendered soul retains her helplessness. No sudden perfection is given, and the soul sees itself as weak after its offering as before; but it must continue to do everything with increased fidelity. It is true that what the soul does remains infinitely little, but it is placed in a new perspective. This infinitely little is no longer illusory but becomes very precious, since it is all that the soul can do to prove its love. These worthless nothings are precisely what call down Merciful Love into the soul. The soul must unceasingly nourish itself by its fidelity in little things, thereby allowing the divine life, in which it desires to move freely, to flow into it.

The heart which surrenders itself at every moment thus penetrates the depths of things; it is determined to put into every action all the intensity of love that the Holy Spirit wishes to communicate to it. The heart desires to accomplish perfectly the duty of the present moment, to unite itself as closely as possible to God. It knows that, whether important or trivial, pleasant or distasteful, in exterior work or interior struggle, the duty of the present moment is the good pleasure of God.

---

[21] S.S. p. 192; Ms. C, fol. 35 r°.   [22] S.S. p. 139; Ms. A, fol. 78 r°.

Does not this realistic attitude make the best use of God's gift and render it most productive? No lost hours, no fruitless graces, no indifferent acts. In tranquillity or activity life deepens; the inner man grows toward the perfect stature of Jesus Christ.

Such fidelity is not attained in a day. No matter, replies Thérèse, falls are not important in this way. Little children's frequent falls never harm them much and do not offend their parents.[23] It is enough that they humble themselves for their imperfections and the grace of God returns in all its strength. "In an act of love, even if not felt, all is atoned for and more."[24]

It is not necessary that the outcome of the effort be successful. Although it has not reached its goal outwardly — a virtue to be practiced, a sacrifice well performed — it has nonetheless reached its deep and essential end. Failure humbly accepted, if it induces a gaze upon Love, activates this Merciful Love, ever stooping to our weakness. "It fills me with joy to have been imperfect," Thérèse admits to Celine. "Today the good God has given me great graces; it is a good day!"[25] Little souls are not required to ascend even "the first step of the stairway" to perfection; they are asked only "to keep lifting *their* little foot."[26] This touches God's tenderness, prompts Him to take in His arms the soul belonging to Him and to carry it in one bound to the summit of sanctity. Love at once erases all that is not pure in the soul; love quickly consumes all that displeases Jesus. "Since that happy day," writes Thérèse, "it seems to me that love penetrates and surrounds me; it seems that at each moment this Merciful Love renews me, purifies my soul and leaves no trace of sin in it."[27]

Thérèse has seen her Sisters wince at their faults and make correction impossible, because they wished to get rid of them more through self-love than to please God. Now that she has given Love the direction of their souls, the saint leads the novices gently and wisely, teaching them not to be troubled by their tendencies toward evil, but simply and firmly to resist them when they are perceived and then to peacefully place themselves again under the radiance

---

23 N.V. p. 89.   26 S.S. p. 293.
24 L. p. 67.   27 S.S. p. 149; Ms. A, fol. 84 r°.
25 M. p. 25.

of Merciful Love. Thérèse asks them to believe unreservedly in this purifying action. Since God has taken charge of their souls, He will accomplish His work in them,[28] provided they never voluntarily turn from Him. He Himself will be their holiness; the rest will be given to them in addition.

They must remember that no virtue belongs to them.[29] Surrendered souls neither acquire nor possess anything by themselves. If they practice all the virtues, and better than others do, it is through a pure gift of God; it is even, in a sense, through a gratuitous loan of love. They should not allow it to distract them from God, and they may not glory in it. Love gives virtues to those souls who look only at Him and live only for Him. It is by truly abiding in Love that they practice virtue almost unconsciously. How good it is for generous souls to understand this! For them the search for perfection, the anxiety to acquire virtues is so often a subtle obstacle, a deceptive blind alley!

In order to put her novices on their guard, Thérèse teaches: "To be little is not to attribute to ourselves the virtues we practice, nor to believe ourselves capable of anything, but to recognize that God put this treasure of virtue into the hands of His little child to make use of it in time of need but it is always the treasure of the good God."[30]

She also reproves her Sisters when they try to get "a supply" of virtue.[31] This attitude of dispossession is so fundamental with the saint that one day, when her patience is admired she protests: "I have never had patience for a single moment! It is not mine! You always make that mistake."[32] She was not mistaken.

Surrendered souls receive everything at each moment from Merciful Love. Simply, like spouses, they dispose of the wealth the Lord is pleased to give them; finding them completely occupied with Him and dispossessed of themselves, He no longer fears that they will become proud. Neither faults nor defeats are obstacles to His work. One thing only can suspend this work or impede it: a soul's attributing something to herself or relying on her own strength.

28 Cf. Phil. 1:6.
29 Cf. N.V. p. 88.
30 N.V. p. 88.
31 S.S. p. 134; Ms. A, fol. 76 r°.
32 N.V. p. 101.

That is the meaning of what is probably the most astounding confidence by the saint to Mother Agnes:

"Mother, if I were unfaithful, if I committed even the slightest infidelity, I feel that I would pay for it by frightful troubles and I should no longer be able to accept death."

"What kind of infidelity do you mean?"

"A proud thought voluntarily entertained, as, for example, this one: 'I have acquired such a virtue, I am certain of being able to practice it'; for then this would be depending upon my own strength and when that happens, one risks falling into the abyss."[33]

To receive whatever will assure our deep fidelity, we have only to expect everything from God. Therefore, confidence and humility are the fundamental dispositions of truly surrendered souls.

In this very simple way "which so enlarges the heart,"[34] as Thérèse's novices say, are there not great exterior sufferings, severe interior temptations, anguish? The saint's example is a sufficient answer:

"To offer oneself as a victim to Love," she says one day to arouse a lazy novice, "is to surrender oneself without reserve to the divine good pleasure; it is to expect to share with Jesus His humiliations and His bitter chalice."[35]

But to another, more timid: "Why are you afraid to offer yourself as a victim to Merciful Love? If you were surrendering yourself to divine Justice you could be frightened. But Merciful Love will have compassion on your weakness; He will treat you with gentleness and with mercy."[36]

Sister Marie of the Sacred Heart expressed the same fears, and Thérèse assured her "that she would not suffer more, but that she would suffer in order to love the good God better for those who do not want to love Him!"[37]

According to Sister Genevieve, the saint repeated: "There is nothing to fear in the offering to Merciful Love, for from this love one can expect only mercy."[38]

---

[33] N.V. p. 89.
[34] Circ. p. 37.
[35] S.S. p. 211; Dep. of Sr. Marie of the Trinity at the Apostolic Process. Sum. No. 1. 358 p. 506.
[36] S.S. pp. 211–212.
[37] M. p. 91.
[38] M. p. 92.

These thoughts complete each other and express the whole truth: surrendered souls are not exempt from sorrows and tribulations, but God sends them because, knowing they have given themselves, He will strengthen them to bear His action. Thérèse affirms this just as much in her trial against faith as in the great physical sufferings of her last months: "Oh, Mother, never have I been so conscious of how sweet and merciful the Lord is. He sent me this trial just at the moment when I had the strength to endure it; sooner, I think it would have plunged me into discouragement."[39] And during her illness: "The good God gives me courage in proportion to my sufferings . . . He will, if they increase, increase my courage at the same time."[40]

If she preferred Carmel "in order to suffer more,"[41] she is more detached at the end of her life: "I no longer desire either suffering or death and yet I love them both. Today it is abandonment alone which guides me."[42] Crosses may come and the answer is found; it is always the same: all is love, the grace is there.

Death itself will be simple. It is, above all, a last act of faith, the bound into Merciful Love for eternity. There is nothing to fear. "It seems to me that for the victims of love, there will be no judgment; rather, the good God will hasten to recompense with eternal delights His own love which He sees burning in their hearts."[43]

The little way is a rapid way. For souls who are open and truly surrendered there is swift progress. Not that they attain the summits at once but, being freed from all the entanglements of natural activity which ordinarily disturbs or retards the divine action, they move at God's pace. Even trials no longer present any real difficulties; there is no need for lights or explanations. God Himself, in His goodness, gives to His children at the moment when they need it, the assurance that they are not deluding themselves, that His love is at work in them and will lead them to the end.

So Thérèse has neither disappointed her novices nor the expectations of God. She has truly brought to a complete fulfillment the

---

[39] S.S. p. 158; Ms. C, fol. 7 v°.   [42] M. p. 195.
[40] N.V. p. 99.   [43] S.S. p. 311.
[41] M. p. 147.

desire to love which she found in their souls; she has satisfied, as far as was in her power, the desire to be loved which she discovered in our Lord's Heart.

All who were entrusted to her and who were faithful have blossomed forth. In giving itself to Love, nature dies to be born again in God. A surrendered soul attains to the fullness of its blossoming, the more generously granted because it has never been directly sought. Since nature acts only under the influence of grace, the natural faculties, progressively freed from all which binds or contracts them, are strengthened and dilated.

Leading her Sisters on this way, Thérèse forged solid instruments of redemption which the Lord, as Master, may use. In the service of the Church they find their meaning and effectiveness. Souls constantly surrendered become divinely active. Whether they are apostles through prayer and love only, or whether they add exterior works to these, what does it matter since they do the will of God! "What Archimedes could not obtain . . . the saints have obtained in all its fullness. The Almighty has given them *Himself, Himself alone,* to lean upon. For a lever, the prayer that inflames with the fire of love . . . thus do the saints militant raise this lever and thus will the saints to come raise it also, even to the end of the world."[44]

Their whole life profits from the Mercy which we know is at work — and at what depths! — in our souls and in our world. Their life is also an imitation of the life of the Most Blessed Virgin who, by her *fiat,* was the first to surrender to Love for His work of merciful redemption.

[44] S.S. p. 194; Ms. C, fol. 36 r° and v°.

CHAPTER VII

The Movement of Abandonment

THE movement of abandonment which, to the theological soul of our saint, is akin to breathing, is fundamentally simple. The purpose of the analysis attempted in this chapter is to make the modern soul more conscious of its riches and to prevent two possible misinterpretations.

1. The movement of soul does not in any way constitute a psychological process in which the entire donation of oneself to God would serve as an excuse for a secret surrender before the reality of life. Far from being a flight from concrete demands, it implies, on the contrary, a full awareness of the obstacles and a complete reliance on God, in meeting them. By this movement every trial, as well as every joy, is transformed and becomes a test of the theological virtues. "With what sweetness I have returned my will to Him! Yes, I wish Him to possess my faculties in such a way that I no longer perform human and personal actions but actions completely divine, inspired and directed by the Spirit of Love."* Thérèse's abandonment, therefore, has nothing in common with an abandonment of ease; it does not cover any hidden psychologism.

2. In another connection the movement of abandonment, far from being a substitute for a true act of faith — that is, faith as an objective return to God — by its very nature gives faith the most prominent place, almost to the extent of making it exclusive. In this it conforms to the pure doctrine of the Gospel.

Unless misused in natural quietude, which is denounced, faith

---

* S.S. p. 318.

is substantially greater not because it is based on a more confident will but because it is more naked and pure.

The more genuine the practice of abandonment, the more clearly one perceives the will of the Father and the presence of Jesus the Savior in every event.

In showing us how to follow the way which she has just marked out for us, Thérèse neglects none of the fundamentals of all spiritual life: who man is, who God is. God is a Father always disposed to forgive. He has spoken to us through His Son who, to save us, has abased Himself unto us. And Jesus has revealed the profusion of His love for us by confiding us to a mother, His own.

The saint has no illusions about man. Without being pessimistic she always brings us back to our imperfections, faults and wretchedness; she is not unaware that this weakness varies in individuals and that each one reacts in keeping with his character; each is a child in his own manner. With what tact and care Thérèse directs her novices! She does not write in the same manner to her "spiritual brothers"; she discreetly adapts herself to their personal dispositions and to actual circumstances.

The counsels which she gave to souls whom she directed must sometimes be changed, but we must always keep the spirit which dictated them and the spiritual axis upon which they hinge. Thérèse is certain that this spirit of childhood can be the mainspring in every circumstance.

But from the beginning one must not falsify it; this imposes a patient apprenticeship. Having passed through this apprenticeship herself, Thérèse, better than anyone, knows how to remove the counterfeits of abandonment, how to teach us to live "in the arms of Jesus"[1] in all circumstances and how to submit with childlike docility.

1. Deviations to Avoid

Under the pretext of abandonment the soul could withdraw into itself and allow deceptions and bitterness to rise within it.

In the face of temptation or natural deficiency it is not a matter of denying the obstacle, of bypassing it as if it did not exist; nega-

[1] L. p. 205.

tion does not put an end to reality. Besides, such an attitude could not last long and might lead to disaster; it causes repression and, one day, the whole hard block of united tendencies confronts the soul. Thérèse puts her Sisters on guard. Sometimes they think they can travel at top speed through the stages of the spiritual life, and suddenly they find themselves as poor as before in the face of accumulated difficulties. Thérèse, who faces trials in order to oblige herself later to entrust them to God, brings us back to the lowliness of our condition: a child does not try to deny his limits; he makes them the springboard of his confidence.

Another temptation lies in wait for souls: to escape. Weighed down by daily cowardice, they lack generosity to return to God in prayer. To stay before Him peacefully waiting would be to offer Him a very weary and heedless heart. Then, too, God's gaze weighs more heavily upon them than the burden of their poverty. Too weak to make a total surrender to the Father, too proud to consent for long to an intimate conversation which might censure them, they take refuge in some absorbing activity which distracts their interior gaze upon God, while allowing themselves the alibi that they are working for His glory. We must not abandon God; we must be transformed.

The saint does not fail to recall: "You must detach yourself . . . from your personal task; conscientiously use the prescribed time for it but with freedom of heart. I read at one time that the Israelites built the walls of Jerusalem working with one hand and holding a sword in the other. It is a good image of what we should do."[2]

It would be a grave mistake to encourage our inclinations or natural desires by offering them a false spiritual nourishment; then, instead of transforming them, we would be subtly maintaining them. Actually, the soul would continue at their level instead of ascending. It is well to warn those temperaments who let themselves be caught so easily, for these merely natural acts are worthless in the eyes of God.

Some souls believe they tend toward God when, in truth, they seek only themselves. Nothing is clarified or purified in their personality. How many times must Thérèse expose her Sisters' egoism

---

[2] M. pp. 100–101.

or rouse them from this narcissism, which they maintain under beautiful pretexts! Such a teacher does not allow them to indulge in tempting illusions: "I do not despise profound thoughts which nourish the soul and unite it to God but for a long time now, I have understood that we must not lean upon them and think perfection consists in receiving many lights. The most beautiful thoughts are nothing without works."[3] The saint relentlessly uncovers reality and brings to light the natural inclination which animates her novices. All these more or less conscious compensations and pleasant returns to "self" are not in keeping with spiritual childhood. This requires a true recognition of our nature and of the difficulty, which is not so much to conquer our nature as to accept it, not so much to rise above it as to offer it to God.

2. The Proper Rhythm of the Movement of Abandonment

If these reefs are to be avoided, it would be a mistake to attack the obstacles; the child does not persist; he calls his father. Rightly, Thérèse would borrow from childhood, not the child's engaging attitudes, artlessness, untroubled ignorance — still less the naïveté — not his humility and frankness, too embryonic to be truly virtuous, but the child's "condition," his "state" of extreme dependence, in which the little one waits for the strength and protection of another to whom he owes his life. What does it matter if the soul falls continually, overcome by weariness and miseries! Perfection remains possible, if it does not become disheartened. Here the Thérèsian answer interests not only consecrated souls but all generous souls who desire to give pleasure to Jesus, for the movement of abandonment is suitable to any circumstance. To see it in its simplicity is to be convinced of that.

If the soul wants to live in abandonment, it must not remain at the "level" of the difficulties that it meets. The movement rightly consists in freeing oneself from the earthly to turn toward God. Instead of battling with temptation or wanting to triumph by itself, the soul immediately rises toward its Father and relies upon Him; better still, it offers the difficulty to Him. When a task appears beyond its strength or means, the soul hastens to take refuge in

[3] S.S. pp. 171–172.

God's arms. When it is not possible to fly over the obstacle, the soul is content to pass "beneath it,"[4] but always in a spirit of confidence and oblation.

In this movement of abandonment that the saint advises for us, those familiar with the doctrine of St. John of the Cross have easily recognized the famous anagogical act recommended by the Mystical Doctor, to permit the soul to rise above all created things.[5] Leaving all behind, it clings to God as by the beat of a wing, as one may speak of the movement of flight. If useless things are in question, the soul forgets all, in God; if necessary affairs are concerned, she sees all in the divine light and accomplishes all in His strength. Everything is thus inexorably brought back to God; the soul leads a theological life. Because the soul spontaneously rises toward God in detaching itself from all, the Lord receives it and communicates His own life to it. Indeed, the soul moves in faith but, as the saintly Doctor says: "This movement is inspired by love."[6]

The art of Thérèse lies in having lived this doctrine in every detail of her life and having given us a concrete and attractive translation of it, enabling us to avoid the painful groping which so often discourages the most generous.

3. Progressive Experience of the Movement

Experience taught Thérèse that this movement does not achieve perfection in the first attempt; practice is necessary. Reflecting upon herself, the saint recognizes that Jesus formed her little by little. Despite her advice and their good will, her young Sisters are tempted by their failures to give up the struggle. She must bring them back to it and teach them to walk, step by step, in the way that she points out to them. Having recalled her own apprenticeship, she can make the way easier for others.

At her own cost Thérèse has learned that we do not react spontaneously by a gesture of abandonment, that we do not im-

---

4 Cf. M. p. 49.

5 The Complete Works of St. John of the Cross, Doctor of the Church, trans. from the critical edition of P. Silverio de Santa Teresa, C.D.; edited by E. Allison Peers; 1943 London, Burns Oates. Vol. III, p. 310.

6 *Ibid.*

mediately give to God the trial which suddenly appears: "One evening, after Compline, I searched in vain for our little lamp on the shelf reserved for it. This was during the great silence and therefore impossible to ask for its return. . . . I realized that a Sister, thinking she had taken her lamp had taken ours, which I needed badly. Instead of feeling distressed at being deprived, I was very happy, realizing that poverty consists in seeing oneself deprived, not only of pleasant things, but also of necessities. In the exterior darkness I was enlightened interiorly. . . ."[7]

This incident shows a disposition. It requires great self-mastery to excuse the religious who made the mistake; we can guess the natural reaction. The interior vexation during an hour of solitary inactivity may very easily continue during Matins. Thérèse reduces the drama to its right proportions and allows herself to be invaded by grace, which purifies and consoles her. It is much more God who comes to her than Thérèse examining her act; her charity, obedience, and patience gently surrender her to the action of God. If we do not here have the movement in perfection, Thérèse seems to have truly understood it in its complexity, after 1890, when her Profession was delayed:

"I must wait for eight months more! At first it was very difficult for me to accept this great sacrifice but light soon came into my soul. . . . One day during prayer I understood that my ardent desire to make my Profession was mixed with a great self-love. Since I had given myself to Jesus to give Him pleasure, to console Him . . . I should not compel Him to do my will instead of His. . . . Then I said to Jesus: 'O my God! I do not ask You to let me pronounce my holy vows; I shall wait as long as You wish, only I do not want my union with You to be postponed through my fault.' "[8]

This text exactly describes the movement of abandonment. Conscious of the trial and suffering because of it, the soul, instead of being rebellious, seeks the cause of her sorrow and discovers it in her pride. She turns to God to adhere to His Will by accepting the affliction and offering it to the Lord for whatever length of

---

[7] S.S. p. 132; Ms. A, fol. 74 r° and v°.
[8] S.S. p. 131; Ms. A, fol. 73 v° and 74 r°.

time it may please Him. Abandonment does not exempt one from effort. Thérèse will direct all her attention to enriching her nuptial robe.[9] This simple fact gives us enough detailed analysis to distinguish the successive operations which the movement of abandonment maintains in the soul. They are: clearly seeing reality, accepting it, offering it.

Thérèse has just practiced abandonment in a particularly crucial moment: could not the Superior's persistent refusal signify God's refusal? This heroic act must be renewed often, even in the most humble circumstances. Sister Genevieve tells us of an insignificant occurrence that taught this to Thérèse:

"One evening during the silence, they had her prepare a night lamp for the outside. . . . 'I had,' she confided to me, 'a violent struggle. I murmured inwardly against the persons and the circumstances; I felt resentment toward the extern Sisters for making me work. . . . But suddenly light came into my soul; I imagined that I was serving the Holy Family . . . and then I put much, much love into it, as I walked with a light step and a heart overflowing with tenderness. Since then I always use this means. . . .' "[10]

In this little incident, which probably occurred in the autumn of 1892, we are given a clear understanding of the reaction of Thérèse, who also wished, in telling it, to influence her sister.

The *Autobiographical Manuscripts* and *Recollections* show that this movement of flight becomes natural to Thérèse. Let us be content with admiring the manner in which she endures her frightful temptations against faith:

"At each new occasion of combat, when my enemy comes to provoke me, I conduct myself bravely; knowing that it is an act of cowardice to fight a duel, I turn my back on my adversary. I run to Jesus and I tell Him that I am ready to shed my blood to the last drop to affirm that there is a Heaven. I tell Him that I am happy not to enjoy this beautiful Heaven on earth."[11]

Here again Thérèse offers us another description, in a new light. Its full significance must be well understood if we are to know the secret of her victories. We must not face the adversary as if

---

9 S.S. p. 131; Ms. A, fol. 74 r°.   11 S.S. p. 157; Ms. C, fol. 7 r°.
10 M. p. 133; cf. N.V. pp. 43–44.

we could crush him by our own weapons; to vie with the enemy alone is to assure him the victory! Thérèse, on the contrary, flees from the combat and casts herself into the arms of Jesus, and by that very act she is on the side of the Victor. ". . . in all these things we overcome because of Him who has loved us."[12]

In order to defeat the enemy with confidence, she recommends the glory of the triumph to God. It is the anagogical act placed within everyone's reach, since one need only accept and offer the temptation in order to give to God the victory. Who cannot conduct himself in like manner?

4. The Nature and Structure of the Movement

As Thérèse arrived at perfection only by an unwearying fidelity, she knows that she has to teach how to repeat this act of abandonment that it may become spontaneous. If some fail, it is because they have neglected a phase of this movement, and have desired to go too rapidly, or have insisted too much upon one beat of the rhythm. Thérèse teaches that abandonment does not increase our wretchedness but frees us from it by our recourse to God. Circumstances oblige her to stress each aspect of the movement, and her collected counsels give a better understanding of the principles which govern true abandonment. This analysis of them, however, must not let us overlook the organized continuity which Thérèse attached to it in her spontaneous flight toward God.

FIRST STAGE

To begin with, the soul in difficulty should look at the situation objectively, without altering it or denying it. Thérèse realizes that her sadness at her delayed Profession is, rather, the result of wounded self-love.[13] If a novice is annoyed because of a preference the Prioress shows to another religious, let her not go to set forth her unappreciated affection: "It is not our Mother whom you love but yourself."[14] To be sure, we are not always responsible for our state: "It is a great trial to see the dark side of things but that does not depend entirely upon you."[15] Nevertheless, if we are sometimes dis-

---

[12] Rom. 8:37.

[13] S.S. p. 131. Ms. A, fol. 73 v°.

[14] S.S. p. 174.

[15] S.S. p. 296; L. p. 245.

heartened by our temperaments, excusing ourselves would be too easy a solution. "When we commit a fault we must never attribute it to a physical cause such as sickness or the weather but admit, without ever becoming discouraged, that this fall is due to our imperfection."[16]

Thérèse thus clearly distinguishes between the state which we cannot control and the act for which we are responsible. She does not seek to avoid an attack of scruples in forming too liberal consciences; the delicacy of her love for Jesus knows no compromise. The demands of God remain, but the sinner need not grieve "in a corner."[17] He should go to the Father who pardons everything, and he should not fear to plead guilty, since he thus obtains divine mercy. Abandonment must live in unreserved humility; we shall never see our weakness too clearly. Thérèse obliges her novices to see themselves as they are. When Sister Genevieve insists rather sharply that some old, worn blankets should not be shaken too vigorously, her Mistress asks her: "What would you do if you were not charged with mending these blankets?"[18] It is also useless to dramatize a situation to win sympathy or to show one's emotions; everything must be in its right proportions.[19] You glory in a praiseworthy initiative? How would you have reacted if it had been imposed upon you? For "there are always ifs and buts when other people's ideas must be adopted."[20] To remain objective in every circumstance, the saint brings us back to our misery. Is this to discourage us?

SECOND STAGE

Not at all! Thérèse wishes to free us. Conscious of her helplessness, she hastens to acknowledge and accept it. Man must not flee from himself nor dislike himself because he is miserable and poor; still less is he to enjoy his ulcers. It is sufficient for him to have patience with himself and not aggravate the evil.

---

[16] S.S. p. 303.
[17] Ms. B, fol. 5 r°.
[18] M. p. 36: "Then when you called attention to the fact that they are easily torn, you would do so impersonally, and then there would be no thought of self in the matter."
[19] Cf. M. pp. 8–9.   [20] M. p. 174.

She finds in her misery a source of joy: "I am not grieved at seeing that I am *weakness* itself; rather, I glory in it and I expect each day to discover new imperfections in myself."[21] "I admit these lights on my nothingness do me more good than lights on faith."[22] If she presents herself in her poverty, God will be obliged to intervene. "I experience a very great joy, not only in being judged imperfect but especially in feeling that I am."[23]

Why should she grieve because of the unfavorable opinion of others, since she herself shares it? The others have reason; why be upset by so distressing a state, since it invites the paternal intervention of the Lord? Her spiritual poverty nourishes and stimulates her hope. That souls are afraid of their poverty grieves Thérèse: "How few there are who accept failure and weakness, who are content to see themselves on the ground and to be found there by others."[24]

In her letter to Sister Marie of the Sacred Heart, she summarizes her teaching in this image: "We need only endure showers patiently; if we get wet, it can't be helped."[25]

In describing the movement of abandonment we have distinguished the obligation of conscience and the acceptance of our limitations. Thérèse does not always explicitly exercise this accuracy, but it must not be ignored. The most important point is to be persuaded of our frailty (first stage) and to accept it (second stage).

Again we find the gospel tones of the Thérèsian message opposed to all Pharisaism, and we hear the echo of the sentiments of St. Paul: ". . . Gladly therefore I will glory in my infirmities. . . ."[26]

THIRD STAGE

It is not enough to accept ourselves as we are; we must offer ourselves. Thérèse's skill consists in preventing the soul from falling back upon itself by encouraging its flight toward God. The very word abandonment, so dear to Thérèse, seems to retain only the passive meaning of the movement of flight. But without this offering, what would our acceptance signify? Now in practice Thérèse strongly insists on the flight toward God. Yet here Thérèse's

21 S.S. p. 170; Ms. C, fol. 15 r°.   24 M. p. 24.
22 S.S. p. 170; cf. N.V. p. 98.   25 S.S. p. 294.
23 S.S. p. 300.   26 2 Cor. 12:9.

teaching may be misunderstood as rigid and uniform; her very flexible method adapts itself to all circumstances and to all states of the soul.[27]

For the beginner in the apprenticeship of abandonment, it is better not to flounder in the situation which makes him suffer. He can return to it later to analyze the matter calmly. For his first attempts let him be satisfied with a rapid glance which will prompt him to cast himself without further delay into the arms of the Victor. To go into the matter, to dwell too long on self or on the suffering would result in discouragement.

"Very often we give only after deliberation; we hesitate to sacrifice our temporal and spiritual interests. That is not love. Love is blind."[28]

When Thérèse suggests to Sister Genevieve that they renew their childish exploit "to pass beneath the horse," she comments: "To pass beneath things is not to look at them too closely, not to reason about them."[29] We must not let ourselves be hypnotized by the adversary who draws us into his camp, but we must free ourselves as soon as possible. The novice may tell her little worries but only when there is no longer "a spark of passion." Above all, the soul must abandon itself to God; later, it can reflect "coldly" on the occurrence in order to know itself better.

The moment comes when the soul, under the influence of grace, acutely perceives the impurity of its motives. Better than any examen of conscience, God reveals to it its limitations and frailty. The soul must not at this time linger in self-scrutiny. Light is given to the soul that it may surrender itself to the purifying fire of divine love. Far from being discouraged because it suddenly sees itself more unsightly, the soul must rush to God to prove to Him that it accepts itself as it is.

[27] In his book on St. Thérèse of the Child Jesus, Van der Mersch is to be praised for having placed in relief the importance of and acceptance of self-knowledge. Because he has said too little about this third step, which is indispensable in the saint's view and which consists in surrendering all to God, in hoping for all from Him, he has falsified the general perspective of the Thérèsian doctrine.

[28] M. p. 70.

[29] M. pp. 49–50; "We were at a neighbor's house at Alençon; a horse blocked the entrance to the garden. . . ."

Thérèse has the wisdom to recognize the work of God. When the Sister no longer needs help in seeing herself, her wretchedness and failures, Thérèse is never lavish with natural consolations to clarify the picture, nor does she ask for purely human effort in self-correction. More than ever one must cast oneself on Jesus. As we have seen, Thérèse interrupts a conversation with a novice when the bell rings for prayer, to oblige her to turn to God. Another takes pleasure in her sadness: "How shameful it is to spend time trembling instead of going to sleep on the Heart of Jesus."[30] Sister Genevieve comes to her to grieve: "I shall never be good!" "Yes, yes, you will succeed," she answers. "The good God will make you succeed."[31] The principle never varies: immediately and unremittingly abandon oneself to God.

When one is faithful to this light on her weakness which God gives her to draw her, she flies to her Father instinctively, with a single "stroke of the wing."[32] Toward the end of her life Thérèse can no longer react in any other way. Supported as she is by the Gifts of the Holy Spirit, she considers it an infidelity to linger too long in a purely natural mood. If her counsels on charity take such a depth, it is because she never goes to others without bringing them the love of God, just as she no longer goes to her Father without carrying her neighbor to Him. "Sometimes we are so badly off at home, in our interior, that we must go out promptly. . . . In this case I see no other way than to leave self and go visit Jesus and Mary in works of charity."[33]

The same act must be renewed in every circumstance. The saint has given the example during her illness; the most insignificant detail, even that which is agreeable or convenient to us, should be an occasion of our turning toward God: "While thanking Him, I found it simpler to offer to the good God whatever I found to my taste."[34] If nature is in command, if the spirit has not had time to take immediate refuge in God, Thérèse does not grieve about it: "In spite of my initial feeling, I repeated to God that I loved Him more."[35] Every fall brings her to the feet of Jesus

---

30 L. p. 323; S.S. p. 296.
31 M. p. 27.
32 M. p. 75.

33 S.S. p. 316.
34 N.V. p. 120.
35 N.V. p. 114.

and her greatest victory is to offer her momentary infidelities. "I hasten to say to God: 'My God, I know that I have deserved this feeling of sadness; nevertheless, let me offer it to You as a trial which You have sent me through love. I am sorry for what I have done, but I am glad to have this suffering to offer You.' "[36]

What is most important in abandonment is the summit. To offer oneself to God in one's present state is the basic disposition at the beginning as well as at the end of the spiritual life. It befits the repentant sinner, as well as the greatest saint. To return to God, to resign all into His hands may often require long training and one must travel, without tiring, the way which we have just traced, in imitation of Thérèse. She has left us texts which allow no doubt on the continuity of the movement, from the awareness of conscience to the abandonment which springs from the humble and sincere acceptance of our limitations.

*

*　　*

NOTE: Miss E. Saint-Pierre, who specializes in Examinations in Psycho-synthesis, comparing this analysis of the movement of abandonment to her own discoveries, has been drawn to make the following remarks which she was willing to convey to us. They clarify and define the psychological processes of abandonment.

"Our generation is reacting against the exclusiveness of the role previously given to the will. The will's mission was that of enforcing the views of the intelligence, save on the impressionable plane when it became an obstacle. It is now recognized that the sensibility should be harmoniously used to carry out what the will decides.

"Thus before a joy or a trial, the proper attitude would be, not to force ourselves by strength of will to a given behavior, but, discounting the immediate subjective human reaction, to regard the matter objectively, taking this as our first reaction, then from that position to face the end or the ideal chosen; that is, to compare the conduct which urged us to follow this first reaction, to that which was evoked by the chosen end or ideal.

"Then we can see ourselves as we are, accept ourselves as we

---

[36] N.V. p. 26.

are; this permits us to strive for our goal and for our transformation into what we want to be. Our threefold summation depends upon intelligence and perception. The three points correspond to the three stages of the movement of abandonment mentioned in this book.

"First: We are *to recognize* the frustration or satisfaction of our feelings.

"Second: We are *to accept* this frustration or this satisfaction of our feelings and face our ideal or our goal.

"Third: We are *to assume* and *to offer* the suffering of this frustration or the joy of this satisfaction.

"Result: joy, interior peace, liberation and freedom."

*

* *

5. Specific Unity of This Movement

Let us cite some instances which will better show us how the three stages, isolated in the analysis, are found again in a flexible synthesis in all the saint's reactions.

"Thinking of the sorrows and the sufferings which await me," Thérèse says, "I arise all the more joyous and courageous; in them I foresee more occasions of proving my love for Jesus and of earning my children's livelihood."[37]

She confides to Sister Genevieve: "I prefer to be unjustly accused because I have nothing to reproach myself for and I offer that to the good God with joy; then I humble myself in the thought that I was certainly capable of doing that of which I was accused."[38]

Here the order is reversed. Thérèse immediately proceeds to God, either by instinct or because she mistrusts her weakness; instead of loitering she hastens to God. Then she comes back to herself, in order to humble herself but not to defend herself. The same conduct is advised for her companions: "Rejoice, therefore, that by letting you feel your weakness, the good Jesus gives you the opportunity to save a greater number of souls for Him."[39]

In practice Thérèse will act with great tact to instill in her Sisters the habit of this flight to God. At one time she will leave

[37] S.S. p. 308.   [38] M. p. 20.   [39] S.S. p. 309.

a novice entirely to herself to "compel her to expect nothing from the human side but to have recourse to the good God to see her faults and to humble herself."[40] At another time she will be more maternal. Later, the only consolation that she will bring will be the reminder of the one imperative necessity: one must fly to God.

Thus, Sister Genevieve, disturbed by a sick Sister's demands, came to Thérèse: ". . . who greeted me lovingly, consoled and encouraged me. . . . 'I understand perfectly that this costs you. . . . Oh! I should have been happy if this had been asked of me! Nature might have found it costly but it seems to me that I would have acted with much love thinking of our Lord's words: I was sick and you ministered to Me.' "[41]

In speaking of a detail of duty, the same religious analyzes Thérèse's method of instruction: "Instead of trying to remove our difficulties by destroying their cause, she made us face them.[42] For example, if I said to her: 'It is Saturday and my companion at work, charged with filling the woodbox this week, has not remembered to do it and I am so careful when it is my turn,' Thérèse tried to make me see what made me indignant. Without denying the black picture I painted for her or trying to brighten it, she made me consider it even more closely; she seemed to agree with me: 'Well, let us admit it! I agree that your companion has all the faults that you attribute to her.' She acted thus so as not to discourage me. Then, working on this foundation, she gradually succeeded in making me love my lot. She even made me wish that the Sisters would be lacking in consideration and kindness toward me, that my companions would fulfill their obediences imperfectly, that I should be scolded in their place or accused of doing badly something that was not even my duty. Finally, she would establish me in the most perfect dispositions. When this victory was gained, she would cite me some unknown examples of virtue in the novice whom I had accused. Soon resentment gave place to admiration and I thought that others were better than I.

"Furthermore, if she knew that the famous woodbox had been filled by this Sister since my visit to it, she took care not to tell me, although this disclosure would have ended my struggle at

---

[40] Cf. S.S. p. 318.   [41] M. pp. 140, 142–143.   [42] M. p. 8.

once. But when she had followed the plan which I have just traced and had succeeded in putting me in perfect dispositions, she would tell me simply: 'I know that the bin is full.' Sometimes she would allow us the surprise of a similar discovery and thus profit by the circumstance to show us that very often we are upset for purely imaginary reasons."[43]

Yet the most vigorous and moving document that St. Thérèse has left us on abandonment is, without doubt, the letter addressed to Reverend Mother Marie de Gonzague, re-elected Prioress on March 21, 1896. In it she gives us both the method and the practice of her little way.[44]

It had taken no less than seven ballots for this election; it is easy to imagine the feelings of the Mother Prioress, bewildered by the troubles which she suspected in her community. Thérèse waited three months before writing. Better than anyone else, since she had received her confidences, she sensed her Mother's confusion. To console her Thérèse prayed, doubtless wishing that others might have the glory of restoring peace to hearts. But time passed and nothing changed. Thérèse felt that she must speak. No duty could be more costly to her; it is necessary to reconcile respect and truth, firmness and sympathy. Who will be able to do this? Jesus!

At once Thérèse leaves it to Him. He will intervene; from Him alone will the Prioress receive encouragements, as well as reproaches. By recourse to Jesus, Thérèse frees her judgment, while she intimately shares the sufferings of her Prioress. Close to Jesus she becomes the advocate of her "Shepherdess"; the tact and the smile of the "lamb" dominate the scene.

The Shepherdess must be led to yield to the reasons of the Good Shepherd, but when the feelings are all agitated, how can Christ be heard? Nature must be calmed.

Thérèse outlines the first steps of the movement which should slowly, patiently, bring the soul into the peace of God. As usual the "little lamb" desires the Shepherdess to fully face reality and not be blind to the truth. She is now living in torment over that which Jesus, nonetheless, willed and prepared from all eternity. Since it constitutes a "chosen trial,"[45] she must accept it without putting

---

[43] M. pp. 8–10.   [44] L. pp. 269–274.   [45] L. p. 271.

the responsibility on others. Thérèse does not permit evasions; the Prioress could have thought that this difficult re-election revealed an invasion "of the spirit of the world."[46] Nothing of the kind, declares Thérèse; this pretext blinds the soul. The Prioress might be tempted, wrongly, to no longer trust anyone, nor rely on anyone, but this would be to go to extremes in what is not conformable to the design of God. This passage is too important not to quote it; it testifies to Thérèsian realism in spiritual direction.

(It is Jesus who speaks): "I did not say to separate oneself completely from creatures, to despise their love, their thoughtfulness, but, on the contrary, to accept them as so many steps, in order to give Me pleasure; for to withdraw from creatures would have only one result: to go and lose one's way in the pathways of the world."[47]

Persistently the "little lamb" prevents the Shepherdess from lingering over views that are too human in order to adopt "divine views."[48] But, then, could not the grieving soul receive an illumination, a heavenly word which would calm her? No, "if I spoke, the trial would disappear";[49] the Shepherdess must live with it.

Thérèse can now make her ascend further steps. She has stated the problem precisely, freed it of all human elements or deceptive artifices. The trial now stands in all its nakedness; the suffering is purified. This is the moment to accept it. Thérèse works with her usual tact. We have observed her keenness of mind in detecting all subterfuge; here we must admire her apt discernment in making the Shepherdess accept the trial. Persuaded that our Lord "does not wish to remove it from her,"[50] she must understand that this cross comes to her from heaven and not from creatures. It is a gift from Jesus to His privileged ones, which should become "a suffering loved and gratefully received."[51] The Prioress will eventually rejoice in thus sharing the humiliations of Jesus. Unceasingly, insistently, Thérèse attempts to convince her that there is no other solution: a generous soul cannot escape the will of God.

From that time on, the Shepherdess will be capable of ascending the last steps of abandonment. Thérèse does not say the word,

---

46 L. p. 272. 48 L. p. 270. 50 *Ibid.*
47 L. p. 273. 49 L. p. 272. 51 L. p. 273.

perhaps too simple and too candid for this person who was not formed in the same manner, but, practically, Thérèse asks her not to remain at this stage of resignation, where she risks retiring within herself and suffering still more; she must surrender to God. Jesus assures her that He has sent this trial "only to fill this loving heart";[52] briefly, to transform her charity in the fire of His love. She must, henceforth, "attach herself to Him alone";[53] all her hope must rest in God, who alone can vivify; and Jesus repeats the words of Psalm 83, "Blessed is the man whose help is from me."[54] The movement reaches completion in the offering of the whole being to divine love.

The secret of Thérèse's prudence and delicacy is in her faithful, often heroic, practice of the movement of abandonment, summed up in a now famous principle: "Holiness does not consist in this or that practice. It consists in a disposition of the heart which makes us humble and little in the arms of God, conscious of our weakness, but boldly confident in the Father's goodness."[55]

To unite us to God, Thérèse, therefore, proposes a way which does not require profound knowledge or human greatness, but which permits every soul to aspire to holiness, once she accepts herself as the Lord has made her. To submit to these laws of abandonment is to walk with assurance, for it is to live in abnegation, to destroy all paralyzing self-seeking and to continue, through the care of souls, in a spirit of redemption. Thus the movement of abandonment remains realistic and true because its laws respect our nature and oblige us to live solely "in the arms of God."[56]

The life of spiritual childhood is not one of ease. Abandonment is not sought in order to relieve suffering but in order to live well in it. We can truly surrender ourselves to God only if we are detached from all self-seeking; generally, the gift is purified in immolation.

The renunciation Thérèse asks of us is the most distasteful to our nature for, constant and hidden, it attacks what is closest to our hearts. Is it a question of worries or of preoccupations? A too

---

[52] Ibid.
[53] Cf. L. p. 273.
[54] L. p. 273; cf. Ps. 83:6.
[55] N.V. p. 78.
[56] Cf. S.S. p. 175; Ms. C, fol. 22 r°.

natural activity which troubles the soul must be renounced; it is better to pray than to torment oneself with useless thoughts. Does an unchecked tendency wish to be satisfied? We must say "no" to the created and "yes" to God. If it is a question of a fault or our sinful state, we must become peaceful, so as to receive everything from divine mercy, expecting nothing from self. If it is a matter of our limitations and our powerlessness, we must humbly accept the fact that we cannot change immediately; we must surrender to Love to be consumed. To renew this detachment throughout the day, the soul needs a rare strength; it takes much courage not to do battle, when it would be more natural to confront the danger. In this way, however, Thérèse wishes to prove her love for Jesus, and it is through sacrifices that all must follow her, for only "the entire immolation of self can be called love."[57]

Throughout these pages we have seen that Thérèse's counsels can serve many souls because she has known how to remain very close to their daily difficulties. She proved the value of her "way" among her Sisters, whose needs made her express her thought clearly. Thérèse requests a missionary not to leave this road; and she puts a seminarian at peace, strengthening him in surrender. Likewise, she discreetly directs her sister, Leonie, who has returned to the world; she foresees that her message will be useful to a "great number of little souls."[58] If the Lord has permitted her to leave us her testimony, it is to enlighten souls who would be disheartened by other paths. Thérèse encourages and stimulates them because she respects the basic nature of the problem, God's supernatural values and our most generous aspirations.

Listening to Thérèse, we often forget her age and her illness, her era and her environment, the sometimes painful conditions and details of her religious life. She herself never disregarded these humble contingencies of which her days were woven; she was never dragged down by them but always used the occasions to rise toward God. Instead of hindering her, they served her spiritual ascent. Always at grips with daily difficulties which impede the flight of the soul, Thérèse never deviates from her initial plan. Not content with using cares and anxieties to go to God, she casts

---

[57] E. p. 26.   [58] S.S. p. 208; Ms. B, vol. 5 v°.

them into the arms of her Father that she may be completely detached. Thus she remains of our world without denying her vocation.

To remain faithful, Thérèse returns unwearyingly to the way of abandonment which lives on all the supernatural realities communicated by God. We have already seen how this movement, unceasingly renewed, is linked to the whole Thérèsian doctrine. Through abandonment Thérèse receives the lights from God to live in faith in Merciful Love. Abandonment, under the influence of divine charity, inclines the saint to offer herself to this Love, so that waves of infinite tenderness may flow into her heart. Abandonment summarizes her whole thought; it requires one to live as a little child, poor and unprovided for, but certain of being loved by a Father who wishes to be its truth, its riches, and its love. Truly, abandonment best exalts the kindnesses of God who "has first loved us,"[59] for it is concerned less with giving than with receiving, less with acting than with surrendering.

Thérèse submits to such poverty only to better free the immense aspirations of her heart. She has so many graces to obtain that she must use the most effective means, the most powerful lever: love, which expresses itself in abandonment, the fruit of spiritual childhood. Thérèse remains amiable and smiling because "love is from God";[60] abandonment permits her to draw unceasingly from this source of living water for the benefit of her confreres. When she sacrifices herself, she always thinks of the innumerable souls of sinners in need of salvation. Thérèse is aware of the tremendous tasks incumbent on the Church, and she is confident of doing much for these intentions. The Gospel assures her that heaven will not limit her activity.

There is no task, no disposition of mind which cannot be returned to God; there is no emotion, no psychological state from which the soul cannot be detached by confiding it to Him.

Whoever is her disciple consents simply to being a poor child, living in the arms of its Father, and leaving to Him every anxiety, every occupation, every difficulty. Sheltered "in the arms of God"[61]

---

[59] 1 Jn. 4:10.
[60] 1 Jn. 4:7.

[61] S.S. p. 175; Ms. C, fol. 22 r°.

or beneath Mary's veil,[62] Thérèse faces storms without fear, for her Father gives her at "each moment" what she needs.[63] Formed by such a teacher, the soul who follows the laws of abandonment is certain of success because, in the consciousness of its utter poverty, it surrenders itself to the conquests of Merciful Love.

[62] P. cf. "The Queen of Heaven to Her Little Mary."
[63] S.S. p. 134; Ms. A, fol. 76 r°.

CHAPTER VIII

The Heart of the Church

WE HAVE endeavored to follow Thérèse in the progressive discovery she made of evangelical childhood and in her teaching of it to the novices, in the course of daily circumstances.

The following pages show how this "little way," which had already brought the saint to complete abandonment, the perfection of love, placed her at the same time in the heart of the Church.

From her youth Thérèse wished to become a great saint and draw after her the greatest possible number of souls; she believed in the reality of our Lord's call to all men: ". . . be perfect, even as your heavenly Father is perfect."[1] Though cares, riches and pleasures of the world may stifle the Savior's words, they will not pass.[2] To those ". . . who were once enlightened, who have both tasted the heavenly gift and become partakers of the Holy Spirit, who have moreover tasted the good word of God and the powers of the world to come,"[3] it becomes impossible for them to escape the thirst for the living water; they disdain the passing things of the world for the eternal realities. Having sorrowfully experienced the emptiness of the world where despair confronts the progress of science, sounding each day the depth of their own sinfulness, many Christians today better understand that only God can effect salvation, though by the most disconcerting human means. They have a realization of their personal part in the redemptive work of the Church, linking the bonds of matter and spirit, of the loved creature to creative love. More than ever the true friends of God must speak; God must be restored to the world and the world to

---

[1] Mt. 5:48. [2] Cf. Mt. 24:35. [3] Hebr. 6:4–5.

124

God. Only those who have identified their lives with Christ the Mediator, only those whose generous and upright hearts believe in God, can do this.

As soon as he wishes to live and work in depth, the Christian is invited to correct his too human vision, to move in God's sphere and to work through Him. Providentially, the "little way" gives us a spiritual attitude concretely embodying in our life this striving toward God. Synthesizing in a single movement aspirations, the diversity of which often rends us, Thérèse opens the way for us: we must develop a theological heart and live the Gospel in the heart of the Church.

1. The Theological Heart

The theological heart, first fruit of abandonment, is a divine manner of seeing, willing and reacting: ". . . he who cleaves to the Lord is one spirit with him."[4]

This divine manner of seeing is founded on faith. Everything comes from God; we have life in Him only by reason of our voluntary dependence: "Because he has regarded the lowliness of his handmaid."[5] Once the Father and His Son are recognized by the soul as the unique value, life, time, trial and even the sorrows of the Church take on their fullest meaning, which is love. The soul then sees the world and herself in a lasting and intimate relation to Him who alone is the Most High. The Father's goodness to the soul corresponds to the welcome given Him, since "God is light, and in him is no darkness";[6] the darkness cast on Him is ours. As soon as the soul depends upon God alone — which dependence is proper to faith in the scriptural sense of the term — as soon as He becomes her all, her means and her end, she shares in His fruitful changelessness and peace; immediately there begins in her, through Jesus, and in Jesus, the mystery of a human heart invaded by God and gradually transformed into one greater than itself. ". . . he who loves me will be loved by my Father, and I will love him and manifest myself to him."[7]

---

4 1 Cor. 6:17. 5 Lk. 1:48. 6 1 Jn. 1:5. 7 Jn. 14:21.

Each day man seeks, by the movement of abandonment, to become established in an adherence of a courageous faith, even to become enamored of the mystery of divine things, which enlightens and guides him better than all human knowledge. "Lord," he may say, "I no longer know but You know for me; I no longer see but You see for me; I no longer love but You love in me."

This manner of seeing all life in God conditions our *will* and all our living forces. When suffering comes, this mysterious divine teaching deepens our certainty that beyond this visible world, Jesus waits for us in another life to say: "My turn now."[8] "Yes," says St. Thérèse, "the Lord will do marvels for us which will infinitely surpass our immense desires!"[9] "He has always made me desire what He willed to give me."[10] Nothing is impossible to those who are not without hope.[11]

Jesus has told us: the Father's heart is always moved by the confidence of His child, but evidently we do not dare to live by the Gospel revelation. The world's greatest sin seems to be the fear of God; if we really believed in His love, we would be less astonished at His power. To hope only in God for ourselves and for the Church, to expect everything from Him and, above all, Himself: this is the condition of happiness. Man, however, remains a prisoner of the selfish need to reduce everything to his own proportions even, and especially, the gifts of God; and the Father is bound by these pretensions. We have the tendency to take to heart only what we see and feel; but God is entirely the Other, He whom we do not understand.

Jesus is the Truth for our faith, He is the Way for our hope, but He is also the Life for our *love*. We are easily convinced that love is the foundation and the end of perfection, but too often we forget that it is the means to it. Thérèse's heroism reminds us of this. Not only will we be judged on love, but even now our love, acting in the smallest things, places us among the friends of Jesus: "You are my friends if you do the things I command you . . . these things I command you, that you may love one

---

[8] L. p. 220.
[9] L. p. 337.

[10] L. p. 351.
[11] Cf. 1 Th. 4:13.

another."[12] Friendly neutrality is insufficient before the gift of God: "he who does not gather with me scatters."[13]

There is, indeed, a constraint of love which is the sweetest of freedoms: if we love God, we must walk in His presence. The act of abandonment, in making us one with the will of God, removes all resentment to this necessity of self-forgetfulness.

"It is love alone that counts."[14] Indeed, all is said, since love is the sole leaven of existence, especially in its Marian and Thérèsian character, deepened to fidelity by the flight to God. Fidelity, the human mark of love, is love which endures. Thus did the Incarnate Word consider His love for the Father: ". . . I do always the things that are pleasing to Him."[15]

What Christ divinely expressed in each of His acts and which He has left us as a spiritual testament, we must imitate, in mystery, throughout our lives, because to interpret the absolute we have to devote all our time to it. We must want God because He is God, intimate love, exclusively and totally gratuitous; we must keep our souls orientated in everything toward Him alone. With the delicacy of a St. Thérèse we must love in advance even the least among His creatures, in common with creative Love who makes lovable what He loves and who seeks nothing in the beloved except the possibility of giving Himself to her.

Faith, hope and love, all converge toward the tranquil depths of our being, which constitutes the theological heart. All our powers are recollected there by the Holy Spirit, who brings us back to a strong and loving attention to the active presence of the Father, and to an intimate communion with His Christ. This is the most complete expression, always possible, of our supernatural activity.

To be sure, abandonment remains a virile struggle; finding God never excuses us from improving ourselves, for we do not approach His holiness without discovering our great needs. God is the only Saint and, therefore, the only One who sanctifies. When He works in us, it is always in His way and according to His thoughts, which are not ours.[16] In abandoning ourselves to Him we do not cease to be wayfarers or escape the sad paradoxes of the Christian. If love

---

[12] Jn. 15:14; 17.   [14] N.V. p. 135.   [16] Cf. Isa. 55:8–9.
[13] Lk. 11:23.   [15] Jn. 8:29.

has crucified the Lord should we be surprised that it rends us apart? Things do not change in relation to us; bathed in faith, we change in respect to them; we approach them from within, from God's point of view, in His will. St. Thérèse has not brought us a new order of holiness where graciousness would replace heroism, but an echo of revelation. There is no Father without children; if God is love we are beloved. It is simply a matter of our not being behindhand.

The great suffering of abandonment is precisely this consent to the gift of God, and the greatest joy we may give Him is to hold out our hand that He may give to us. Theologically, man sees his positive values change in meaning: to give is to receive. Furthermore, if we can now proceed toward the possession of God, it is because God first came to us in His Son and "because God first loved us."[17] Our noblest efforts will ever be but a response, and this is the basis of the beatitude of the poor in spirit. Certainly divine grace, far from suppressing our nature, perfects it; God respects our liberty too much to disregard our consent. But if He advances at our pace, He keeps the initiative. Faith, which is man's consent, is also a light from God. Hope, which is human confidence, is, in the first place, divine kindness. And charity, before being our gesture, is the movement of the Holy Spirit. The strength of God thus takes possession of human frailty. All the great prophetical missions of both the old and the new alliance have known in their beginning this necessary forsaking of human selfishness, which releases the full power of God. Only in this light of divine transcendence can the thirst of all theological souls for humility be understood. The characteristics of love are humility and obedience unto death. Jesus willed to live in poverty and dereliction, amid kingly joy, so we also should do.[18] When Thérèse speaks of herself as little, it is not a childish complacency but an objective view of her relationship with God. If He is All, she is nothing without Him; nevertheless, she can do all things with His grace.

This is the road to the summits, the way that forms true Christians, that obliges us to ascend toward happiness with a strength

---

[17] 1 Jn. 4:19. [18] Cf. Jn. 13:15.

which is not ours. It is a theological short cut, adapted to our human weakness, in which Thérèse has discovered the face of love in God's demands. Besides, so profound is the repercussion of the movement of abandonment on our psychological being that it compels us to admire the power of the Holy Spirit, giving us, through the saint's spontaneous words, a synthesis that is both human and doctrinal.

A theological heart is, first of all, the source of a great liberation from all negative feelings of doubt, bitterness or despair which poison our supernatural atmosphere. "The truth shall make you free."[19] We know that: "There is therefore now no condemnation for those who are in Christ Jesus."[20] For: "Coming, he announced . . . peace to you who were afar off, . . . peace to those who were near,"[21] and "through him we both have access in one Spirit to the Father."[22] "Perfect love casts out fear."[23] Thérèse's message is the logical commentary of these words of the disciple.

The logic of love seems difficult. It frees us, however, from narrowness and greed; a child possesses nothing and is little concerned about defending his rights. He begs affection and has the happiness of receiving it naturally. A theological soul does not know what it is to make reservations; confidence is sufficient for it. Its total fitness for the sole "office of love"[24] frees it from the constraints of the times, in keeping with the Lord's explicit desire in His prayer of the Our Father, following the pure and free flight to God: "Father, hallowed be thy name. Thy kingdom come!" Jesus successively takes from us the yoke of the present: "Give us this day our daily bread," the remorse for our past: "forgive us our sins," and the anxiety for the future, in which His grace will triumph: "and lead us not into temptation." Man now has a heart sufficiently enlarged to live the eternal in the world, without being of the world. In the measure in which God is free to act in the soul, the soul is free for God.

Then an astonishing change occurs as the Holy Spirit takes control of the natural faculties; at the heart of this divine intimacy, the soul possessed by the Spirit of Jesus attains to the fullness of

---

[19] Jn. 8:32.   [21] Eph. 2:17; cf. Isa. 57:19.   [23] 1 Jn. 4:18.
[20] Rom. 8:1.   [22] Eph. 2:18.   [24] Cf. L. p. 285.

existence. Its intelligence, will, and imagination act only under the influence of grace, are dilated, spiritualized, and freed of all that limits or troubles them. This transformation of the personality is a normal gratuitous consequence of union with Christ; it is the more fully granted to the soul because she never directly sought it, since, solely for a motive of love, she renounced everything. Thus transformed, the soul frequently remains unaware of the change effected in her by the divine contact. Generally, it is only others who enjoy her human and supernatural fullness, while she continues to live in complete self-forgetfulness. She is aware of the divine life and also of her total dependence on God.

Purified by His hidden presence, we gain a fruitful knowledge of ourselves and our limitations, which the current of modern thought sometimes repels. Instead of making us rebellious, this knowledge brings us to a sane realism, where hope fills the voids of man. We discover the fullness of the Paschal mystery of death and life into which the Lord has plunged us, and the profound meaning of human history. Because we are at last placed before God, the world and time are attuned in us. Our own existence, however disappointing it may be, already has a celestial value, since Christ Himself undertakes its sanctification.

The wonderful unity in a theological heart shares with Jesus the simplicity of God. "Abide in my love."[25] This commandment of the Lord, making known His infinitely loving appeal and offer of unheard-of intimacy, often seems to us remote and sometimes even cruel. How can we remain in Him when life bruises, torments, and uproots us, when weariness and shame make everything look black? Through a single means: Jesus and Jesus alone. This is not a technique but a Person; nor is abandonment any longer a technique, however Christian it may seem, for a technique is always a harpoon thrown into things. We cannot capture God or the, God-Man; we can only see the open arms and throw ourselves into them. How great and mysterious! To see and hope only for God and in God, to want only Him and all things for Him: all life in Christ is here.

Thérèse felt this yearning for unity in God which ennobles man,

---

[25] Jn. 15:9.

but she did not expect this unity through escape from her conditions of life nor through superhuman struggle. She did not break herself. She gave herself: "In order to live in an act of perfect love, I offer myself as a victim of holocaust to Your merciful love. . . . I feel my helplessness, and I ask You, O my God, to be my Holiness."[26]

Following in her footsteps by an act of abandonment substantially the same and repeated on every occasion as a reflex of love, any soul can tend, while still on earth, toward the eternal present where God sees, loves, and awaits her. Each instant then becomes a meeting and little, by little, in the strength and sweetness of the Holy Spirit, the acts of love become a state which will receive the seal of glory in Heaven: "I see what I have believed. I possess what I have hoped for, I am united to Him Whom I have loved with all my power of loving."[27]

Such are the master lines of the theological life in its Thérèsian version, wherein the dynamism of grace seizes, in her poverty, the soul freed by abandonment. The modern world needed this message steeped in revelation, and God has rekindled the hope of thousands from this little flame of Carmel.

2. The Evangelical Heart

The universal radiance of St. Thérèse's message comes largely from the vitality of the Gospel. Beneath the saint's words we find this atmosphere of confidence and humility in which the Lord wished to see souls blossom and without which spiritual childhood is unthinkable.

We must yield to the obvious: Jesus Himself, almost solemnly, has imposed upon His disciples the spirit of childhood, as an absolute condition to the work of sanctification. Very often He affirms this necessity and always in condemnation of pride: "Amen, I say to you, unless you turn and become like little children, you will not enter into the kingdom of heaven."[28]

---

[26] S.S. p. 448, St. Thérèse's Act of Oblation; cf. Appendix.
[27] L. p. 346.
[28] Mt. 18:3.

During an apostolic journey through Galilee Jesus, for the second time, saddened His disciples by prophesying His sufferings: "But they did not understand this saying, and it was hidden from them. . . ."[29] Their petty worries distracted them from these tragic revelations. "And they came to Capharnaum. When he was at home, he asked them, 'What were you arguing about on the way?' But they kept silence, for on the way they had discussed with one another which of them was the greatest."[30]

This was wholly "the reasoning of their heart":[31] ambitious dreams instead of the reality of the cross; before He was dead they were dividing the inheritance! Jesus said nothing. He sat down, called the Twelve; then He drew a child to Him, a little one, no doubt frightened at being among all these men, and too surprised to be proud. Jesus embraced him. Who is the greatest? The littlest. Who is the first? The last of all, the servant of all. With one gesture Jesus swept away all our false importance; the unimportant child becomes the model. God chooses what is not to confound what is.

Notice that Jesus seems to keep only one quality of childhood, humility: "Whoever, therefore, humbles himself as this little child, he is the greatest in the kingdom of heaven."[32] The Master knows very well that He is dealing with man: "Unless you turn,"[33] He says, which supposes that He takes them as they are with their weight of years and selfishness. We are not concerned here with a poetic emotion but with a complete returning to spiritual perspectives: to become, by gradually forgetting ourselves, as little children.

Mothers knew well the Lord's fondness for little ones; He, on His part, willingly lent Himself to their requests: "They were bringing the babes also to him that he might touch them,"[34] "lay his hands on them and pray."[35] The Twelve, scolded once before a child, "rebuked them,"[36] as though in thrusting them aside, they could evade the demands of Jesus of which these little ones were the living parable. "But when Jesus saw them, he was indignant, and

29 Lk. 9:45.
30 Mk. 9:32–33.
31 Lk. 9:47.
32 Mt. 18:4.

33 Mt. 18:3.
34 Lk. 18:15.
35 Mt. 19:13.
36 Ibid.

said to them, 'Let the little children come to me, and do not hinder them, for of such is the kingdom of God.' "[37]

And the Master completes His lesson: "Amen, I say to you, whoever does not accept the kingdom of God as a little child will not enter into it."[38] Children's humility consists in this: they accept their having to receive. They, at least, know the gift of God and surrender unconditionally to the love which comes to possess them.

Remaining with the Synoptics in this severe affirmation of the Master, we are as uneasy, no doubt, as the disciples; whatever uproots our self-complacency always seems unreasonable to us. But the conversation with Nicodemus related by St. John leaves us firmly united with the intentions of Jesus, compelling us to follow Him on the supernatural plane where all His spoken words are made clear. The psychological context is identical; again man, conscious of his worth, raises objections to a paradoxical demand of Jesus: " 'Amen, amen, I say to thee, unless a man be born again, he cannot see the kingdom of God.' Nicodemus said to him, 'How can a man be born when he is old? Can he enter a second time into his mother's womb and be born again?' "[39] This is, indeed, the major objection to spiritual childhood: why impose childish reactions on an adult? The old doctor protests with some humor: a man is born only once! "Jesus answered, 'Amen, amen, I say to thee, unless a man be born again of water and the Spirit, he cannot enter into the kingdom of God.' "[40]

All spiritual childhood is contained in these calm sentences of Jesus. As we cannot enter the Kingdom without being born again of water and the Spirit, with this new birth we must grow in love. Spiritual birth corresponds to childhood in the Spirit. Meanwhile — and this is the essential contribution of this new text — neither one stops with the human image, always needy. "That which is born of the flesh is flesh; and that which is born of the Spirit is spirit."[41] Jesus speaks of birth: God is Father and He begets; Jesus wishes us to be children so that He may have us abide in God as divine children. These realities of birth and childhood must

---

[37] Mk. 10:14. [39] Jn. 3:3–4. [41] Jn. 3:6.
[38] Mk. 10:15. [40] Jn. 3:5.

be lived in faith and mystery. Jesus asks of us, as of Nicodemus, a flight into the invisible: *"Do not wonder that I said to thee, 'You must be born again.'* The wind blows where it will, and thou hearest its sound but dost not know where it comes from or where it goes. So is everyone who is born of the Spirit."[42]

Values do not give way to the absurd; Jesus simply shatters their limits, transfiguring them in His own vision. Childhood, which in natural life is only a transitory state leading to adulthood, becomes, in the sphere of grace, the ideal state, the final flowering of the whole spiritual destiny. The Christian will no longer strive to pass beyond this new childhood but to tend toward it; and only a death of love can establish him in it. To be a child in the Spirit is to prolong indefinitely the unique act by which the Father gives us His life in Jesus; it settles us "for life" at the very source of our Baptism. From this flows our greatness of sonship, our fundamental dependence, our grandeur and our humility.

Each time Baptism creates a son of God, a spiritual childhood is begun. When the water, symbol of the Spirit, flows onto our forehead, we receive the Kingdom as an unparalleled gift of God. God acts in us; we let Him act in us and we let ourselves be acted upon. Spiritual childhood invites us to continue this attitude of helplessness and waiting for God by giving it the character of trial. "Crave, as newborn babes, pure spiritual milk, that by it you may grow to salvation; if, indeed, you have tasted that the Lord is sweet."[43]

Having found her way in the Gospel and having meditated at length on our Lord's Passion, Thérèse could not forget the true condition of our journey toward God. Certainly, we are His children, but ungrateful children, reduced by Adam's sin to the state of paupers and beggars. Not only do we share the condition of the first man, receiving from him a wounded nature and tendencies to evil, but through our own sins we share his transgression. Thérèse knows that the history of man can now only be a history of salvation; with an amazing sureness of intuition, she maintains three essential points in her way of abandonment: man destroyed the plan of creation; the Word Incarnate alone inaugurated the re-

---

[42] Jn. 3:7–8.   [43] 1 Pet. 2:2–3.

demption; and, lastly, we owe our sanctification to God to whom we adhere by faith.

Adam withdrew from the Father; Thérèse wants to come near to Him. Therefore, she must take a direction diametrically opposed to the road on which Adam had fled from love or, more exactly, she must travel that road in the opposite direction and in the light of the Spirit. To the spirit of independence Thérèse opposes her submission. Man had thought himself the master of the earth, whereas it was God who had made it subject to him. He thought he could do without God, to "be as gods,"[44] not understanding that only his obedience could assure him the kingship of this universe. Man rebelled in order to assume a total autonomy; having deprived himself of God, he found he was at war with himself and all creation. Thérèse, on the contrary, wanted to remain a child; she no longer knew how to do without God; she could do nothing and wants nothing apart from Him. Far from freeing herself from the protection of the Father, she sought His yoke and found it light.

Pride is thus cut at the root. Adam, having denied his limitations as a creature, lost God's friendship. Thérèse understood very early the paradox of His power:

> "He rejects pride and takes by choice
> The feeble arm of a child."[45]

The Lord knows our poverty and to pour out His affection He awaits only the confession of our sin and the unembittered acceptance of our weaknesses. Most of all He requires pure hearts to receive His fullness; humility is the path of love.

In Thérèse's soul, where "love alone counts,"[46] selfishness no longer has a hold. By choosing God's pleasure as her sole objective, Thérèse reverses this morbid twisting of man's will which is centered on himself, on his interests, on present deceptive joys. In her there is no eagerness for selfish gain, no feverish pursuit of God. Of herself what can she acquire or give, since everything comes from the Father? "Or who has first given to him, that recompense should

---

[44] Gen. 3:5.
[45] P. "The Shepherdess of Domremy Listening to Her Voices."
[46] Cf. N.V. p. 135.

be made him?"[47] For it is we who own our being to God.

The way of childhood, therefore, effects this return of the spirit which Jesus asks in His first sermon and which is the prelude to entry into the Kingdom. "The time is fulfilled, and the kingdom of God is at hand. Repent and believe in the gospel."[48] "To become as little children" is to empty ourselves of the selfish, sensual self in order to enthrone God in the inmost part of our being. It is to renounce this need, so deeply rooted in us, of being the sole master of all we survey, of deciding for ourselves, according to our whims, what is good or bad for us. Spiritual childhood, then, constitutes the most objective and fundamental answer to Adam's sin. Man separated himself from God in the hope of growing; Thérèse unites herself to God by refusing to grow. Man wanted to be someone, unaided, and he made himself a prisoner; Thérèse chose to belong to Someone and in God she freed herself.

Nothing costs us more than to become a child, even in the spiritual sense meant by Jesus, for the whole struggle of our existence pulls us in the opposite direction, to affirm and strengthen our personality. We must suffer much to become humanly adult and trace out a way for man in a world no longer human! To propose to a breathless fighter the ideal of a badly trained child could be mockery; and perhaps more than any other, our era would answer it by revolt, increasing the irony of Nicodemus to blasphemy. It is important to realize that such a reaction may conceal Christian soundness. God has made our growth a natural law. Of Jesus Himself the Gospel declares that He "advanced in wisdom and age and grace before God and men."[49] Moreover, this growth is presented to us as the first duty of the Son of God: "And the child grew and became strong. He was full of wisdom and the grace of God was upon Him."[50] In the order of nature, as in that of grace, we must leave the swaddling clothes and the stammerings. St. Paul said: "When I was a child, I spoke as a child, I felt as a child, I thought as a child. Now that I have become a man, I have put away the things of a child."[51]

This progressive development, which should lead us to the "full-

---

[47] Rom. 11:35.   [49] Lk. 2:52.   [51] 1 Cor. 13:11.
[48] Mk. 1:15.   [50] Lk. 2:40.

ness of Christ"[52] serves the body as a whole. ". . . I have chosen you . . . that you should go and bear fruit, and that your fruit should remain."[53] Also such a uniform maturing of the Christian can turn only to the glory of God who created by love and for love.

There is no question of an unnatural suppression of every human impulse and enthusiasm. For pusillanimous souls there is a very real temptation to conceal in spiritual childhood a commonplace fear of life or an unconscious flight from adult responsibilities. To go through life as though fording a stream with no more burden than a schoolboy's worries would be easy but unnatural and of little redemptive value. There exists a duty to grow up, for God has committed us to time to earn here in love our freedom. It is not man's harmonious growth that Jesus condemns in the name of spiritual childhood, but a disordered development, at the expense of the one thing necessary.

Nevertheless, in the economy of the Redemption, the attainment of the full stature of Christ is assured — paradoxically — only through a continuous dispossession, the dispossession that the "little way" sets forth. We must constantly rise above the contingencies of our human life, to communicate on earth with the eternal present of the Father who is even now working in us. In our human existence our life proceeds to its completion by the addition of ever richer acts. In the higher perspective of the Kingdom, all the superabundant glory promised us is already developing the seed of Baptism. We need only let God act, humbly and confidently responding to His love at each moment. The Father does not ask us to amass treasures which rust, but daily and in silence to enrich our souls to the dimension of His imperishable treasures.

There can be no contradiction between the growth to maturity which God asks of us, and the condition of childhood in which He wishes us to remain. Spiritual childhood is inactive only in appearance; actually, it is the "coefficient" of humility and confidence which affects each moment of our life. To dwell in God is to grow. That is the miracle of Christian newness drawn from the living water of the torrent of God.

---

[52] Eph. 4:13.
[53] Jn. 15:16.

Jesus knew man and the power of that human pride which nailed Him to the cross. He knew that the Gospel would counteract the sin and that the sinner would one day feel bewildered and helpless. He was not content with pointing out the ideal of childhood; He wanted to be its living example.

All that Thérèse included in her way of childhood, Jesus, who is the Way and the only Child, drew from His filiation. Indeed, only the love between the Son and the Father consummated this childhood in the Spirit. "Now this is everlasting life, that they may know thee, the only true God. . . . But the Father dwelling in me, it is he who does the works."[54]

The whole Gospel is nothing other than the likeness of the Father. This is precisely what Thérèse found there; and, as everything that is revealed of the Father implies a corresponding attitude in the child, the Christian life is sharply engraved by the sole impression of God's image on the soul. Jesus asks us to live as sons, miserable, no doubt, but infinitely loved. Thérèse's "little way" will start at this crossroads of the beatitudes. Joy in abandonment despite trials and the burden of sin, the amazing confidence of the prodigal son and of the blind, the humility of the unprofitable servant: this is the line of conduct which Thérèse has traced from the Gospel.

Several hours before His death, Jesus, the Master and Lord, wishing again to be the Servant of all, knelt to wash the feet of the proud: "For I have given you an example, that as I have done to you, so you also should do. Amen, amen, I say to you, no servant is greater than his master, nor is the one who is sent greater than he who sent him. If you know these things blessed shall you be if you do them."[55] A last beatitude, that of the Servant, the Humble, and therefore of the Child.

When Jesus gave His Body and His Blood as nourishment, even though Judas was already betraying Him, He was at last able to say to His disciples the words which had burned in His Heart for so long a time: "Little children, yet a little while I am with you. . . . A new commandment I give you, that you love one another."[56]

Dying, Jesus has nothing more to give: He had given us all the secrets of the Son. But He also surrendered to us the secret of His

[54] Jn. 17:3; 14:10.　　[55] Jn. 13:15–17.　　[56] Jn. 13:33–34.

Mother, her love and her transparency. Jesus gave us His Mother, not to keep but to look at, because seeing her, we shall know how she saw God, and that alone is important.

In His Servant, God offers us the model of humility; in the Virgin, the model of abandonment. And she who brought God into the world received the mission of bringing us into the world of God and of forming in us the child she was, and the Child she bore. Without doubt we shall never see Jesus more clearly than through the eyes of her who called Him: my Son, the first-born of a multitude of brethren.[57]

3. The Heart of the Church

"In the heart of the Church, my Mother, I will be love."[58] This concise formula which Thérèse has given us as the plan of her whole life can bring to many souls the peace the saint drew from it. Thérèse had a lofty idea of the missionary apostolate and of the extent of the Church. She would have loved to go to distant lands to preach, to convert, to give her blood for the cause of the Lord, like many others the memory of whom was continually present to her. Nevertheless the will of God and her love had enclosed her behind the walls of Carmel. Divine incoherence? Waste of perfume? A Judas would have said so; Thérèse never thought of it.

A prisoner of love, but prisoner by love, she found that her immense desires were never restricted by solitude. On the contrary, for in the desert of this heart-to-heart she attained union with God and became free. Thus the soul of Thérèse shares more and more intimately in the universal redemptive plan. Clinging in silence to the simplicity of God, Thérèse ascends imperceptibly to Him, and she discovers the world from a greater height in the very look of the Lord. At the same time, her field of action was growing, for Jesus was working in her helplessness; in Him she had found her role in the Church.

---

[57] Cf. Lk. 2:7; 48; P. "Why I Love Thee, O Mary."
[58] S.S. p. 203; Ms. B, fol. 3 v°.

For Thérèse, the Church is, first of all, a Mother. Take from a mother her eyes to smile, her arms to console, her hands to comfort, and what is essential to her mission would still remain; she has given life and she loves this life which is part of her flesh.

A mother's heart is an echo: the mother surmises all before the child speaks; she has a presentiment of sufferings, of tears; she reads distress in an evasive glance. No fall astonishes her, no wound repels her, for the bleeding flesh remains a part of her own, and every weakness is an appeal to her love. A mother gives birth throughout her life. This power of compassion and of welcome makes her the living bond of the family; in her are centered the destinies of those whom she has given to the world. Her children leave her and live their own lives, often without thinking of what they owe her. Though they may go on for years without looking back, a mother's solicitude follows, sustains and encourages them; her heart echoes their joys and their hopes.

So, too, the Church. She is at one and the same time a warm, maternal atmosphere where the littlest ones are the most loved, and a home of expansion. Until the end of time the baptized will receive life, light and food through her; and until the return of Christ, the drama and the pride of man will echo in her, as well as the gropings of history. But she can contain and assume all, for the Heart of the Spouse has no other limits than the infinite love of the Lamb.

To live in the Heart of the Church is to be united with her in her extent and richness, her plan of salvation; it is to espouse her fervor and inspiration, her welcome and her mission, which explains in time and space the love of God. Thérèse wished to seize the Church's power of sanctification at its source, as it comes from the Heart of Jesus. To be sure, all baptized, by their personal bond with the Mystical Body, participate in this dynamic reality which unceasingly raises us to the Father. But it is indeed a trait of the saint's spiritual genius to have consciously lived it, and especially to have discovered in it the providential inclusion of all souls, however alone and poor they may be.

To lose her limitations in the Heart of the Church, Thérèse gathers the universality of the atonement into the poverty of her human heart. Deprived of all tangible riches in the field of action and with nothing but her love, she plunges by pure faith into the wisdom of the Father, certain of immediate participation in His power.

Thérèse's success is an appeal for us all. She came to remind us that our sanctification and that of souls in the Church is a continual birth. There is no need to be strong or gifted to be of the Church and serve her cause, to be the light of the world and the salt of the earth. We are not a Church of powerful souls but of sinners and weak ones; Jesus came to save that which was lost. From what crossroads has He not brought us back to eat at the Father's table: the lame, the blind, the disabled? What does it matter! The Kingdom of God knows no other coin than charity. Beneath the nuptial robe all our unsightliness disappears, and things possess in the sight of God only the weight of love which surrounds them.

So, too, in heaven, we have: ". . . not a high priest who cannot have compassion on our infirmities, but one tried as we are in all things except sin";[59] "Wherefore it was right that he should in all things be made like unto his brethren, that he might become a merciful and faithful high priest before God to expiate the sins of the people. For in that he himself has suffered and has been tempted, he is able to help those who are tempted."[60] In the same way our weakness has its part in the "royal priesthood" of baptized souls,[61] in so far as it puts us in union with the hope of the world.

Finally, our apostolic radiation depends much less on the conditions of life in which God has placed us or the qualities of our actions, than on the faith and confidence which lead us to respond promptly to His love. Saved by love, we shall save only by love; this is the supernatural realism which Thérèse has revived for us. She has lived it with the haste and exclusiveness which only the saints have known. Certainly, the Lord freed her very early from every human hold on souls, and thus she could more rapidly stake her life on love alone; but every Christian, in the measure in which he keeps his baptismal innocence and allows himself to be carried away by the Spirit who confirms him, has the same claim on the

---

[59] Hebr. 4:15.   [60] Hebr. 2:17–18.   [61] Cf. 1 Peter 2:9.

heart of Christ. If we are sons of God in the measure in which the Spirit guides us, all vocations converge and complete each other in the heart of the Church, since in an absolute fidelity to grace it is much less a matter of work or contemplation, activity or inactivity, than *to be acted upon* by God.

The role of love that Thérèse played in the Church does not suppress other roles; on the contrary, it presumes them, but it remains indispensable so that the apostles, the witnesses and the martyrs may find in the Mystical Body the strength to hope and to hold out to the end.

To the degree that the Thérèsian doctrine on abandonment is known and lived, it appears as the providential antidote to the poisons of our times. It would even seem, at times, that the young Carmelite had a presentiment of the anguish and needs of our troubled world and that she wanted to embody them in her short life.

Who shall say what enrichment this doctrine still holds for us? It may bring a recovery of health to modern thought, by welcoming the limitations of man and by a determined yes to his condition as creature. Eschatology will gain, no doubt, from contact with this realism which gives value to the liberty of the redeemed and love in the present moment. Already the mystic has made her own the resolutely evangelical orientation of reparative love, which Thérèse bequeathed to her.

The mission of Thérèse concerns all Christians. To those whom God draws to the cloister, she recalls the fruitfulness of apostolic contemplation; to apostles, thrown into the conflict, the primacy of their union with the Vine, of that passivity before God where, in mystery, all deep action subsists — lacking that, how could one, with a contagious faith, speak of the Lord as a friend? To those whom illness condemns to inaction or whom persecution slowly dehumanizes, she brings the certainty of a supernatural efficiency which can make them the greatest in the Kingdom. To all, finally, whatever the burden of their work or its obscurity, whatever their sufferings, Thérèse repeats the universal call to intimacy with God.

Perfection is an astonishingly simple step; all that it asks is faultless fidelity. It suffices to choose God because God has chosen us.

But we must see as He sees and will what He wills. Becoming a saint is not a matter of chance; it is a choice. Thérèse shows everyone the "one thing necessary,"[62] which is to lay hold of the heart of God by a prayer that is without impatience or caprice, in the name and in the place of those who refuse Him; to be in all places and circumstances the divine "transformer," the man reborn of water and of the Holy Spirit, capable of offering men to the merciful regard of the Savior, in order to permit Him to take them unto Himself and give them an eternal name.

Thus did the Virgin act, from Nazareth to Calvary and until her Assumption, ever opening her soul to the unparalleled dimensions of her Maternity. Sanctification will never be only an individual advancement; it is always a work of the ecclesiastical order. One cannot approach the Head without being taken into the service of the Body. And Thérèse, by voluntarily inscribing her vocation in the heart of the Church, her Mother, linked her eternal destiny to that of Mary, who, by her unseen communion with Christ, is the type of the Church and in heaven symbolizes its anticipated perfection. Thérèse's role in the Church is but the crowning of her Marian life. Now that Thérèse is reunited with her Mother in glory, doubtless our Lady has been pleased to entrust a reflection of her maternity to her who has raised up throughout the world a multitude of souls dedicated to Love.

In fact, the only thing that the Lord seeks for His glory and needs for the salvation of the world is ". . . true worshippers . . . in spirit and in truth,"[63] individuals in whom He lives and acts freely, "other humanities,"[64] in whom He can fully renew His Mystery.

---

[62] Cf. Lk. 10:42.

[63] Jn. 4:23.

[64] According to the words of Sr. Elizabeth of the Trinity, *Souvenirs*; R. P. Philipon, O.P., *The Spiritual Doctrine of Sr. Elizabeth of the Trinity.*

Appendix

Penance and Health

RENUNCIATION holds a very important part in the life and teaching of St. Thérèse. She considers it the condition of love.[1] But she seeks less to destroy nature than to render it more pliable to the influence of grace.

Thérèse teaches us to consider everything, first of all, from the interior. The actual, distressing matter of the novices' health should also be considered from this viewpoint, under pain of despairing of the future of the religious life.

Too frequently today's novices have little health, physical strength and nervous resistance. They know it and more or less acknowledge it. It becomes a grave problem for them when, despite everything, they desire to lead a life that is pure, mortified, and really hard. They need the "authentic" and resolutely want to be realistic. In their minds the "authentic" is often identical with the visible or exterior. True poverty, mortification, and austerity mean, for them, what can be seen, felt, and breathed. Let us admit that they are not wholly wrong.

Therefore, it is very painful to these young novices, on the one hand, to lead a life which they think too easy, even mediocre, and, on the other hand, to be obliged to acknowledge that they could not endure a more rigorous one, and that they have difficulty in adapting themselves to the life that is offered them. And when they realize that their strength does not even permit them to keep the common Rule, the deficiency is extremely painful to them. They feel inferior to the older religious who are sometimes capable of doing more than they. Often they fear they may be taking the place of another who would be more suited to follow the Rule.

This is distressing, not only for the Superiors responsible, but for the novices themselves. In her dealings with them, the Mistress must show great delicacy, clear-sightedness, and a knowledge of where she wishes to lead them. Her duty is to see that all the conditions of life, both physical and moral, safeguard health. With the help of competent authors, she must clearly explain what true health is, to what extent one must desire it and how, through mortification well understood, one may try to improve or maintain it.

---

[1] Cf. M. p. 153 and cf. p. 179.

147

1. Health and Its Use

Some novices, as a matter of fact, think that to give themselves totally to God consists in exposing themselves imprudently to all risks, inclemencies, and contagion, and in not concerning themselves about food, cold, or sleep, within the bounds of reason and good sense. That is imprudent generosity — especially characteristic of beginners — which, more often than not, lasts no longer than a fire of straw. Having become accustomed to agricultural work and "hard knocks," the novices are tempted to believe that the more work they do and the more they mortify themselves, the better they will become. They do not consider what is possible to accomplish for a time — and which may even be demanded in Religion — cannot reasonably continue for a lifetime. The Mistress must show them that in acting in such a manner, they will quickly wear themselves out, and will end by falling into a state of depression and anemia, requiring care and dispensations detrimental to mortification and to the religious spirit; a sane prudence would have averted this.

Sometimes, especially in contemplative Orders, there are novices who aspire only to make their Profession, free to remain afterward in the infirmary to suffer and die. But death is not so prompt and a prolonged and demoralizing illness is rarely (so the *Imitation* claims) a means of sanctification for a soul who could not practice virtue in health. On the other hand, as a religious who is ill enjoys neither all the comforts and little treats which the "rich" can indulge in, nor the advantages and spiritual supports of the regular life, she may come to regret having entered Religion or at least no longer understand the meaning of her vocation.

Finally, there are novices who seem, on the contrary, most preoccupied with their health, and who judge everything according to their natural repugnances or their fear of falling ill. They do not really work to conquer themselves, forgetting what they can do with grace. They rest, they spare themselves, under the pretext of some day being able to follow their Rule. As St. Teresa of Avila says: "They seem only to have come to the monastery to work at not dying. . . . Well! The first thing to do is to rid ourselves of the instinctive love of ourselves. There are some religious naturally so fond of their ease that they have much to do here. . . . Therefore, take courage, my Sisters, you have come here with the intention of dying for Jesus Christ and not to treat yourselves delicately for Him. The devil represents to the soul that it is necessary to take care of herself in order to follow and keep the Rule; and then we attend to our health with so much care that we die without having followed the Rule completely for a month or perhaps for a single day."[2]

---

[2] *Way of Perfection*, Chapter X, Trans. E. Allison Peers, *The Complete Works of Saint Teresa of Jesus*, Ed. of P. Silverio de Santa Teresa, C.D. (New York: Sheed & Ward, 1949).

We must avoid, if possible, falling sooner or later into these errors, and to correct them if they exist. Here the Mistress should give the novices a clear, supernatural rule of conduct.

1. Health, like life, is a gift of God. Therefore, it is not to be imprudently endangered. We can also ask for it in prayer, in total abandonment to God.

2. Health consists in a balance, a harmony between the body and the spirit.[3] If this is not understood or cannot be realized, health disappears. However, there are many indispositions which do not really endanger health; they furnish material for daily sacrifices, all the more meritorious because only God sees them.

3. A religious must not desire health for the happiness of profiting by it and being free from suffering, but that she may zealously observe her Rule, serve her Community and devote herself to her contemplative and apostolic work. In everything she must desire the accomplishment of God's will.

4. The health of a religious is not in her hands. God disposes of it and her Superiors have the care of it. She should make known her state of health and answer any questions asked, then submit to the decision which may be made.

During their Novitiate the Mistress is responsible for the health of the novices.

2. The Conditions of Health

It is important that the Mistress place the novices in an atmosphere conducive to a harmony between body and soul. A number of nervous depressions, anemias, and other disturbances, as well as departures from the convent "for reasons of health," are due, in fact, to a multiplying of reproaches, to the requirement of an obedience that is too passive and blind, to overwork and its resultant interior disorder, and to an exaggerated tension, which results from the novices trying to accustom themselves too quickly to the laws and customs of the institute.

In general the Mistress may think that the recent shock experienced by the novices in leaving all they loved, their arrival among strangers, the difficulties of adjusting to the religious life — far greater for the young today than for the former generations — the work of assimilating so much new data, and the interior sufferings, constitute sufficient material for sacrifices, and often cause such psychic turmoil that it is better to avoid their consequences, than to aggravate them by useless and premature demands.

It seems necessary, for instance, to consider that now novices need more time to adapt themselves to the religious life and to grasp the deep meaning of certain observances, than was needed thirty or fifty years

---

[3] Let us note that this harmony may be attained — at a higher level — by those overwhelmed by illness or infirmity. A painful harmony but so rich in love!

ago. The world they leave is very different from the one they are entering, especially for contemplatives. In order to adapt themselves to the work of grace, the time of the postulancy or the novitiate might be prolonged, allowing the adjustment to be gradual and more solid.

The Mistress must do all that is possible to avoid nervous tension. Experience proves that better results are obtained when, upon their entrance, the postulants (and, when necessary, the novices) are given a time of real rest, permitting them to catch their breath again. Qualified doctors cite the lack of sleep as the most common cause of depression in religious. They estimate that, in our hypernervous civilization, eight hours of sleep are necessary for many twenty-year-olds. The time thus "lost" is more than "recovered" by better prayer (it is not normal to sleep at prayer), by a truer, simpler practice of patience and fraternal charity, by superior work and, in a word, by safeguarding mental balance.

Food also requires attention. Certain natures cannot remain fasting in the morning. All have need of nourishment, simple, without doubt, but sufficiently rich and varied.

Certain "breakings," formerly necessary and fruitful, today would actually shatter the nervous and psychic strength of the novices. An atmosphere of confidence, joy, friendliness and noble ideas, with the infusion of true spiritual inspiration, are very real elements of health because they aid interior flowering. In these "hothouses" of novitiates, the Mistress must take great care not to be a screen between souls and God. She will avoid idle conversations and childish talk but will spread joy that expands and dilates, enlightens and nourishes, thus furthering their ascent toward God. Her conferences should be carefully prepared and imbued with life. The report on prayer should be brief, for it is not necessary that they reflect upon and analyze self. Besides, the novices may not have matter for a daily report to the Mistress. She should see that they do not overindulge in long prayers, especially if they become routine. Taking into consideration their intellectual and spiritual formation before their entrance into religion, she will recommend reading appropriate for the needs of each soul, and to the particular appeal of grace and personal culture.

At the same time the Mistress will obtain exterior peace for the novices, a certain unity in work, and the necessary physical exercise (gardening or other)[4] carried out prudently, not in the heat of the day nor — and this is a delicate problem which requires solution — during free time. The Sisters should not usually be obliged to rest from one duty by performing another. Housework always demands sustained energy. Each Sister has her daily share of sweeping, of mending and the charge entrusted to her, without considering the weekly turns in duties, such as the reading in the refectory, serving at table, dishwashing, bell ringing, and so forth, and the unforeseen works of charity, humble services which sometimes consume hours. What is to be said about work

---

[4] Perhaps Swedish or corrective exercises are an excellent ascesis for those uninterested in outdoor activities.

which "brings in revenue," and which tends to become more and more intensified?

It seems, therefore, urgent to compensate for daily fatigue by daily relaxation. Since nowadays it becomes impossible to take this relaxation at the expense of work or sleep, could we not sacrifice, from recreation time, one hour for solitude each day?

The objection might be raised that religious contemplatives, observing absolute silence during the whole day, need to speak during the hours of recreation. Rare is the religious who speaks only at recreations. Her first duty of the day is to get her permissions; then she may have many things to decide with those holding offices. Hardly has the Sister returned to her cell when she may be called: a service to render or ask, supplies to be procured for herself.

Thanks to this hour of free time, Sunday will be relieved of a number of small obligations and become truly the "Lord's day." Reading may be done from a good book, prayer will be intensified, and strength will be renewed for the labor of the coming week. This will also bring the joy of seeing order and harmony in one's life. Once this relief is effected, a joyous ardor will replace "the pressure" caused by an accumulation of unfinished tasks on all sides. Since it is not exactly the work but the multiplicity, the feverishness, the anxiety of always feeling overwhelmed, health will profit by this rest from tension, and the mind, the spiritual life and the observance will gain by it.

Nevertheless, the novices themselves have much to do to maintain their health, and an important problem remains: how to reconcile this necessary balance and the practice of penance, especially in monastic Orders?

3. Penance and Health

Usually novices tend to do more penance than is asked of them, even by God. They dream of an austere and hard life, but certain observances demand a much greater effort from them than from their seniors. For example, they may find the food too plentiful or too well prepared, but they will scarcely touch foods which do not please them, and so forth.

Here, also, we must emphasize the proper things. We must use their need for the "authentic" and their undeniable generosity to make them understand that the most authentic things are the most interior, though they often appear small, even insignificant, because practical and immediate. We must not, with irony and harshness, point out to them the gap between their ideal and their capabilities: they are only too painfully aware of this! But one must profit from this to make them transfer their need of mortification from the exterior to the interior and, at the same time, from the impossible to the possible. They are capable of doing this, and, in reality, it is what God expects from them.

An interior austerity practiced at each moment in minor circumstances is more thorough, more difficult and more meritorious than certain great material sacrifices. To be sure, corporal mortification retains all its redemptive value; the lives of the saints, even the most "human," sufficiently testify to this. To deny asceticism, traditionally approved by our Lord's Church, would be to preach against wisdom and, still more, against the cross of Christ. The hygiene of the body and the soul, the human balance so desirable for the spiritual life — these are not ends in themselves nor the last word of the Christian ascesis; they are the stones waiting for the spiritual temple which God wills to build in every generous soul.

The mystery of Jesus in which we should live each day is death and life — life by death and death for life. It is necessary that the heart of His death must ever beat in our lives in order to diffuse love to the confines of the Church, and joyfully to transfigure our daily death in His glorious life. "So that I may know Him and the power of His resurrection, and the fellowship of His sufferings: *become like to Him in death,* in the hope that somehow I may attain to the resurrection from the dead."[5]

We have, therefore, every reason for distinguishing two planes (which often interfere for the glory of God):

— *the plane of "basic health,"* physical and moral, without which it would generally be foolish to hope for a full Christian development; acquiring it can become a true ascesis. "For which of you, wishing to build a tower, does not sit down first and calculate the outlays that are necessary, whether he has the means to complete it?"[6] More psychological, this aspect deserves consideration because the role of teacher can be decisive.

— *the plane of voluntary participation in the Passion of Christ,* the limits of which are known only to God. "And what is lacking of the sufferings of Christ I fill up in my flesh for His body, which is the Church."[7]

The direction which must be adhered to by the soul can be easily summed up: to follow the Spirit and to ask for counsel. The teacher must be very careful not "to extinguish the Spirit," and to know souls well, so as to judge sanely and reasonably. Exacting and flexible, the Christian ascesis therefore remains, in all cases, eminently spiritual and God-centered.

By interior austerity is meant not only renunciation, detachment of the heart and mortification of self-love — although these are of primary importance — but, more especially, an attitude of soul which tries to raise all things to God. There is more true austerity in an exact silence which does not admit useless contact; in a recollection which avoids a curious glance, does not allow an indulgence in earthly pleasures, and refuses to dwell too long on fleeting impressions. Yes, there is more true austerity here than in exterior penances, where, according to Thérèse, "more of nature than of virtue"[8] often enters. The novices must learn

---

[5] Phil. 3:10–11.
[6] Lk. 14:28.
[7] Col. 1:24.
[8] N.V. p. 77.

to mortify their bodies in this multitude of little things which also mortify their inmost souls. The ascesis of one who tries to deny herself the enjoyment of food that is to her taste, in order to keep all her interior attention on God, is more rigorous and more absolute, without doubt, than that of another who thinks only to resist her greediness.

One must take up one's cross to follow Christ, but the important thing is to follow Him. The cross to be carried is only a means to this.

Unquestionably, in these things it is the inspiration which counts and the love that one places in them; nevertheless, if the novices tend to see only externals, the Mistress will often be obliged to remind them of the more direct spiritual aspect of mortification. True interior discipline, constant in little things and without display or self-satisfaction, calls for great strength of character, a flexible will and a soul already greatly taken by love. To perform punctually all the ceremonies of the choir or those of the refectory, to incline, to rise, to stand straight, or to begin a reading immediately, as soon as the signal is given — all these humble fidelities, these breakings of every moment, prove that a novice is usually attentive to God, surrendered to Him, and that she does not leave much place within herself for caprice and her own will.

Who can say what a firm will and a true command of interior forces can communicate to the strength of the body itself? Mortification is meant to liberate the soul, not to control nor to stifle it in making the body incapable of serving it. Therefore, it would be a deceptive mortification which would oblige the soul to occupy itself unceasingly with "brother ass," to maltreat him. That, too, is being concerned with him. True penance must tend to that by which the body no longer craves a multitude of natural satisfactions; but not to that which makes it groan, overwhelmed to the point that the soul hears only its voice. It is a known fact that too much suffering or even physical fatigue makes prayer and attention to God difficult.

The modern novices can understand this. They say it of themselves. The Mistress should, therefore, encourage them to put it into practice, and to endure without complaining the harmless annoyances resulting from the cold, heat, and the little discomforts of life. Let her accustom them to pay no attention to that which crucifies nature, not to complain about an endurable headache or a toothache, not to put on or discard clothing too soon at the change of the seasons. The body thus accustoms itself more easily to everything, and one avoids the two excesses: to give it too great a place or to expose it imprudently.

The Mistress will put them on guard against self-love in their work, which urges them to do more than they can, to undertake too heavy burdens, to tire themselves beyond measure; they must also avoid laziness and selfishness which leave everything to others. She will show them that it is easy for each one to do, not that which exceeds her strength, but whatever is most disagreeable to her, what the others do not wish to do; such as choosing the most unpleasant place at the washing, like Thérèse; true mortification consists in this.

Finally, as for food, an important point, she will ask them to get accustomed, from the beginning, to eat a portion of everything that is passed at table, to obey in the refectory as elsewhere, to believe that what is commanded of them is possible. They should not consider their likes and dislikes but close their eyes to everything, and think that God Himself sees what is served to them, and that that suffices for them to take it with a good heart. As St. Thérèse said, "Very often it is in the refectory that the most sweet aspirations of love come to me. Sometimes I am constrained to stop. . . . Oh! it ravishes me when I think that, if our Lord had been in my place, before my portion, He certainly would have eaten it. He would have taken what was offered to Him. . . . Then it is very probable that during His mortal life He ate the same food as I."[9]

The Mistress will be very firm in not letting the novices have anything between meals, unless there is a real need; comforts quickly become a necessity when the stomach becomes accustomed to them and demands them; then in the refectory the novices may complain of not being hungry. These irregularities of diet are harmful to the soul as to the body.

Finally, the Mistress will watch that the novices do not let themselves give in to the distaste and worry which is born of interior trials and humiliations or which come from the emotions themselves. Some novices cannot sleep nor eat as the time approaches for their Clothing or Profession, or when they are in trial, or even when the least annoyance is suffered. In these circumstances one must be very emphatic, even sending back to the refectory a novice who manifests undue sadness or the inability to exert herself.[10] Let the Mistress ask her daughters to master themselves and submit, to be unmindful of self in all and for all. By this firmness she will contribute much to balance their temperament, for mortification thus conceived and conducted, far from being harmful to health, stabilizes and strengthens it.

But that should not prevent the Mistress from being solicitous about a loss of appetite or sleep which appears real and which lasts, for this is often the sign of a state of abnormal fatigue or the messenger of serious illness. It is better to call the doctor too soon than too late. On the other hand, it is often necessary to know how to conceal one's anxiety, to ask the novices not to complain too quickly about their small discomforts; and, as much as possible, to discern those who go to the end of their strength without complaint, from those who exaggerate their slightest indisposition.

If she wishes to see her novices, healthy or ill, become true religious,

---

[9] S.S. pp. 306–307.

[10] One knows the incident in the life of St. Teresa of Avila: One evening when overwhelmed by persecutions which threatened to ruin her work, she remained in the refectory, without touching her food. Our Lord appeared to her, took a piece of bread and held it out to her, saying: "Eat, my daughter, this is good for you now."

energetic and mortified, the Mistress will try to place them in an atmosphere of indifference, to make them strong souls who neither choose nor refuse anything, accepting everything that comes to them as coming from God and knowing how to find in everything occasions of mortifying their nature to the benefit of the spirit and, therefore, at the same time, of health.

This hidden combat of a soul who strives to keep herself entirely, including her senses, for God alone and to establish herself above everything that is not God, grants less of a hold to self-love than does the accomplishment, even difficult, of a life exteriorly poor and hard, in which one could glory.

In this the novices of today are truly Thérèse's sisters: at once they are "armed knights," as the little saint said, relating an incident from the Life of Blessed Suso, concerning corporal penances: "He had performed some frightful ones, which had ruined his health, when an angel appeared to him and told him to stop, adding: 'You have yet fought only as a simple soldier; as of now I shall arm you as a knight.' And he made the saint understand the superiority of the spiritual combat over the mortifications of the flesh. "Well, little mother, the good God has not wanted me to be a simple soldier; I was at once armed a knight, and I have engaged in the war against myself in the spiritual domain by abnegation and little hidden sacrifices; I found peace and humility in this hidden combat where nature has no hold."[11]

The way that Thérèse opens is sure and providential. With her one must teach today's novices to sacrifice, not their ideal, but all the externals which they cannot realize. To teach them that is a delicate thing for they should be persuaded immediately that what they cannot give to God must be replaced by a higher and more interior giving and one exercised in little things which are very costly. It is also a most necessary thing, for without this re-establishment of balance on behalf of the spiritual and of the possible, one is exposed to the danger of having novices who are always tense or always relaxed.

[11] N.V. p. 77.

Index

157